RUN LIKE A STALLION

RUN LIKE A
STALLION

How American Football Explains Turkey

RHETT BURNS

Cover design by Rebecca Valerio

Cover photo by Shannon Burns

To my wife Shannon,
I'll go anywhere in the world with you.

To our football players,
HIT LIKE RAM, RUN LIKE STALLION,
WIN LIKE A CHAMPION

Table of Contents

1. This is Turkey...1

2. A Long Way From Tuscaloosa..............................9

Çay Break

3. First Down and Miles to Go............................23

4. Çevre..33

5. European Dreams..47

Çay Break

6. Carpet Fields and Volleyball Knee Pads.................61

7. Twenty-Five Yards From the Ball.......................71

Çay Break

8. Tebowing..81

9. The Fiery Blaze in Taksim...............................93

10. Throwing a Smeagol Tantrum..........................99

Çay Break

11. Football Changed My Life.............................117

1

THIS IS TURKEY

"Twins right seventy-nine arrow deep, on one."

That was the play I called. It's a simple play, really. Two receivers line up to the right and do an X-cross, one streaking down the sideline, the other finding the seam somewhere near the hash marks, if such a thing existed in Turkey. The quarterback rolls right and hits the open man deep. Elementary, my dear Ahmet.

I always go deep on the first play from scrimmage. The opportunity to demoralize an opponent on the very first play is too appealing, like a boxer going for the knockout punch in the first round. To continue the mixed sports metaphors, I like to swing for the fences, and such a baseball reference is appropriate here because of the unique relationship between baseball and football in Turkey. When I tell people in Turkey I am an American football coach the conversation goes something like this:

Me: "I coach American football."

Ahmet: "Oh yes, yes. I know it. Baseball."

Me: "No, no American football. It's the one with the helmets and—"

Ahmet, interrupting and swinging a pretend Louisville slugger: "Yes, yes, baseball. It's boring, but a great social event."

Me: "You're right, baseball can be boring. And it is a great social event, with the food and all. Especially if you get the ice cream in the miniature helmets. But American football and baseball are different. American football is the one with the egg-shaped ball."

Ahmet: "Ooohhh, yes! Of course. I know it. I've seen it in movies. It's such a rough sport!"

Having to analogize the sport you coach to the developing embryos of farm animals is a good indicator of its popularity, or lack thereof. And let's be clear, American football is not popular in Turkey. Yet, a generation of younger Turks, influenced by Western media, have come of age with the gridiron in their peripheral vision and are now focused on making it mainstream. They caught their first glimpse of American football in movies like *Any Given Sunday* or television shows such as *Friday Night Lights*. They first played it on video games. Occasionally they found an NFL broadcast on satellite television. They form a niche of devoted fans and players, not unlike the extreme sports subculture once was in the United States before the X Games made it popular. It is unclear if American football will ever register as mainstream in Turkey.

I say these young Turks grew up with football in their *peripheral* vision because soccer is the point of focus for any self-respecting, patriotic Turkish sports fan. Soccer is the national sport and pastime, complete with all the pageantry and hooliganism that normally attends the sport. As such, opportunity to play and learn soccer as a child is as wide as Anatolian farmland. But no Pop Warner league exists for kids to learn how to block and tackle and "stay deep as the deepest," which is another reason why I like to go deep on the first play from scrimmage. Turkish defensive backs will almost always play the run first because a) they haven't been drilled since the onset of puberty to never let a receiver behind them; and b) they never really had to worry about a deep passing threat, as a deep ball in Turkey typically resembles a high flying, single-winged pigeon. So if you have a quarterback who can sling it—and we did—you can get loose downfield for an easy score.

This is exactly what happened on that seventy-nine arrow deep, the first play I called in a road game against the Mersin Mustangs. Our quarterback rolled right and threw the ball on a zip line to a receiver as open as the nearby Mediterranean Sea is wide. Our receiver caught the ball and strolled into the end zone, which under normal circumstances would have been the early demoralization of an opponent that we were gunning for.

But American football in Turkey is never played under normal circumstances.

The road to Mersin is long and laborious, passing through cities and mountains and vast swaths of nothingness. The trek took us fifteen hours by bus. We could have made it in twelve if it were not for the extra long tea breaks the bus drivers took in the middle of the night. We boarded the bus at 9:00 p.m. so we could avoid the normally hellish Istanbul traffic as well as an extra night of hotel fees. Some players were coming from class, other from work. Much to our delight one player brought his work with us, a cooler full of Magnum Bars, a chocolate-covered ice cream bar that is a giant evolutionary leap from the brown mule bar I ate in elementary school. Others brought recreation with them, drinking beer on the sly in the back of the bus, in direct violation of both Islamic law and our team's "no alcohol 48 hours before a game" policy. As a Turkish teacher once told me, rules in Turkey are just decorations, expected to be excepted and broken.

At first players just chatted with one another on the bus as we made several stops across the city to pick up players. Each player who boarded the bus greeted everyone else on the bus with a handshake or a kiss to the cheek, usually both. The bus driver missed one stop so the he did what Istanbulites do when they miss a turn. He threw the bus in reverse and backed it up the highway, oncoming traffic forced to adjust. We were not too far out of the city when the inevitable dance party broke out. Yes, dancing. Yes, inevitable. As inevitable as cigarette smoke and tea. Traditionally, Turks like group folk dances, but these young Turks demonstrated the effects of globalization and Western influence in their dance. iPhone flashlight applications made suitable enough strobe lights and no dance move was too ridiculous to be performed to the blaring techno music. It was part night club, part Saturday Night Live, part Psy video, and all fun!

But the lights grew dim as we left Istanbul and most fell asleep before we reached Ankara, the capital city that resembles Atlanta in some uncanny ways. Personal space being as foreign a concept in Turkey as free refills and bacon, some players fell asleep draped across one another, or as we call it back home, cuddling. Lest you get the wrong impression, physical touch does not carry the same taboos here as it does in the United States. Friends of the same sex often drape an arm around one another or interlock arms while walking. Sure, it's awkward for Americans, but it means nothing more than friendship. These same cuddle-buddies will suit up in pads a day later and lay a crossing receiver flat on his back or pancake block an oncoming rusher.

The physical touch displayed by Turkish friends is a good illustration of a principle that holds true about a lot of cultural nuances that is important to remember when living abroad: "It is not wrong, just different." A friend who holds my arm and escorts me down the street is not wrong. The practice is just different than the way we do it in South Carolina. Back home I may greet a friend with a handshake or even a proper man hug—you know, keeping our shaking hands between our chests and giving a hard slap to the arm with the off hand. In Turkey, I greet friends with a faux kiss to each cheek. Not wrong, just different.

You will do well to remember this principle while reading this book. I will point out many things that I have experienced that are culturally different. Reading without the proper lens could lead to the misinterpretation that I am making fun of or demeaning Turkish culture in an ethnocentric manner. That is no more my intention than jumping into the cold Bosphorus water beside me right now and getting stung by the gaggle of jellyfish staring me down. No, I highlight the differences because that's what makes living in another country interesting. And hopefully it is what makes reading this book interesting. The differences between our cultures season and add texture to our shared existence like the crushed red pepper you find on nearly every Turkish table.

That said, cultures are not value-neutral. No culture is pristine, neither Turkish nor American, and all cultures need redemption because they are made up by deeply flawed human beings. I am not afraid to make value judgments about some aspects of Turkish life and culture, but not every mention of cultural difference carries such a judgment. So if I write about women standing on ledges five stories up to clean their windows every week, know that I'm not against clean windows or women or women cheating death in order to have crystal clear windows. I just find going to such dangerous lengths to clean windows interesting, not to mention scary. But if I write about the recent news report that over a third of Turkish men find domestic violence against their wives "occasionally necessary," then I am likely calling this behavior, and the heart from which it precedes, wrong. I trust you will be able to tell the difference. I neither intend to give Turkey the rose-colored glasses treatment nor sucker punch my second home by solely pointing out its flaws. Rather, I hope to accurately present the contours of Turkish culture, its glories and its grunge.

Coaching the Koç Stallions American Football Club gave me a front-row glimpse into both glories and grunge. After arriving in Mersin after fifteen hours on a bus, I walked along the Mediterranean coast with friends, eating sunflower seeds—Turkish style, one at a time, cracking shell with two front teeth—and chatting about life, religion, and football. We later settled into a café where a few guys puffed on the smooth, fruity smoke of the *nargile*, known elsewhere as hookah. In a *nargile* café the conversation draws out slowly and calmly, like the tobacco through the water, unlike the tensity of a conversation over cigarettes. We left the café to go eat Mersin's famous *tantuni*, a wrap stuffed with small pieces of spicy meat. Every city in Turkey is famous for something, usually a food dish, and *tantuni* is certainly worthy of its notoriety. Long hours spent with friends in conversation and jest over deliciously prepared local food is one of the glories of Turkish culture. This evening proved to be such, at least until about midnight when our coaching staff experienced some grunge. Several of our players decided it would be a good idea to get high on marijuana the night before a game. Our coaching staff immediately decided to suspend them from the following day's game for breaking team rules, a decision not made easier by our friendship with them. Young men searching for fulfillment in drugs is a grunge to be expected in most any culture, but I must admit I was surprised when it happened with our guys.

The next day we arrived at the stadium a little later than expected because we got lost on the way. When we arrived we were pleased to see a large crowd for an American football game. The Mustangs' coach was a Texan and he had promoted the game into a big local event as Texans are wont to do. The local news sent a cameraman out to catch the event, as this was the Mustangs' inaugural season and the first team in the city. The mayor was in attendance as well. As our team warmed up, our coaching staff met with Mersin's coach. He informed us that they had to switch stadiums unexpectedly and that this one had some quirks. The end zones were seven yards deep and the field, more closely resembling an infield than outfield, was only ninety yards long. If we accepted these dimensions we could play the game. If not, we could postpone the game or perhaps win by forfeit since they did not provide a proper field. Seeing that we slept Friday night like pretzels on the bus for fifteen hours to get there, we elected to play. Winning the coin toss we elected to receive the opening kickoff.

That's when I called, and we completed, the seventy-nine arrow deep. That's when our receiver coasted into the odd seven-yard end zone. That's when the referee blew his whistle and threw a flag in the middle of the play, while the ball was still in the air.

And that's when I about lost my mind.

The Mersin game was only the second or third game of the season so I had not completely adjusted to Turkish officiating even though I had been warned repeatedly. As our quarterback hit the slot receiver down the right sideline, a defensive back knocked down the wide receiver toward the middle of the field. In the middle of the play, as our slot receiver was catching the ball, the referee inexplicably blew his whistle to assess a pass interference penalty away from the ball. The touchdown was nullified, an inadvertent whistle the culprit.

Inadvertent whistles happen, I get that. But that isn't why I almost lost my mind. To compound that mistake they do not even give us the spot of the ball when the whistle was blown, which was about forty yards down field. And then, just when I thought incompetence could not exponentiate to another power, we did not even get the fifteen yards for the pass interference call. Nope, we just replayed the down from the original line of scrimmage. My jaw dropped. I could not believe what was happening. I screamed. I yelled. I pleaded. All to no avail.

So I laughed.

And that's when I learned an important Turkish phrase. *Burası Türkiye*, "this is Turkey." And a second phrase is like it, *yapacak bir şey yok*, which means "there is nothing to do." The implication of these phrases is frustrating to an American who thinks every problem should be fixed and every wrong should be righted. The implication is there are some things that will happen in Turkey that seem so bizarre, so wrong, and though they seem correctable, they will never be corrected. And there is absolutely nothing you can do about it.

So we moved on as best we could. I called another play and ended up scoring on that opening drive. The game moved at an excruciatingly slow pace. In the first half it seemed the officials threw a flag on every play. A false start here, an offsides there. A pass interference 30 yards from the ball sprinkled in there for good measure. Whatever. The first half lasted over three hours. A nasty leg injury to a Mustang player accounted for some of the time, especially as we awaited an ambulance to arrive at the field to replace the one that took the injured player to the hospital. One rule that is not broken is that an ambulance must be at the game or play cannot resume. Surprisingly, no one was injured on the single most bizarre tackle I have ever witnessed. As our running back broke free toward the left sideline, instead of leading with his shoulders and wrapping up for the tackle, one Mustang leaped into the air, positioned himself parallel to the ground, and, leading with his legs, ninja-kicked our running back's legs out from under him.

Burası Türkiye.

We won the game en route to an undefeated regular season. I was glad to survive to fight another day. And I received an education that day about Turkish American football, Turkish culture, and the country that was my new home. I also learned that if you paid attention to the right things this foreign game might just explain Turkey.

2

A Long Way From Tuscaloosa

Turkey is odd, peculiar even.

Turkey is not odd in a bad way. Nor is it odd just because it's different from my own country. No, Turkey is odd because it is different from what one would expect. Turkey is odd because it is incongruent, its history and present chock full of paradoxes and contradictions and tension. Yet, there is a prevailing unity of experience that somehow comes to make sense over time, which I suppose is just another paradox. Turkey's complexity does not make it odd in itself. All nations are complex because, if for no other reason, the human beings who make them up are rarely simple. But Turkey's complexity is visually and experientially striking. The democracy and the Islamism. The religiosity and the secularism. The skyscraper and the village. To this South Carolina boy, it's all very odd. But it is Turkey's complexity—its oddity, even—that makes it beautiful and interesting and important. And at the same time, frustrating. Again, paradox.

Many books have been written about Turkey. These books generally explain the republic using political, religious, and historical frameworks, touching on architecture, food, education, language, and a host of other cultural indicators. I do not doubt the usefulness of these frameworks, but I believe something more subtle—and more fun—can explain much of Turkey as a nation and culture as I've experienced it over the past three years. That *something* is American football. It only makes sense that something as odd and out of place as American football should explain Turkey.

Of course, American football cannot explain everything about Turkey. I will not attempt to do so. For instance, American football cannot fully explain why, after decades of friendship, Turkey nearly severed all ties with Israel after the *Blue Marmara* flotilla incident. Larger geopolitical realities were at play. But geopolitics are affected by everyday people. And these everyday people live their lives from a worldview and culture. And some of these everyday Turkish people play American football, bringing their worldview and culture to the football field. These stories and observations from two years living and traveling in Turkey while coaching the Koç Stallions provide us a general explanation of Turkey, its people and culture. This book is not intended to be an advanced and technical analysis of Turkey, but a fun introduction to newcomers and those interested in a cursory overview of the nation and its people.

I received my education about Turkey on a soccer field in northern Istanbul, where I spent two years coaching the Stallions. True to Turkish complexity that field was sometimes beautiful—on a clear day you had a gorgeous view overlooking the Black Sea—and sometimes horrid—on winter nights the fierce Black Sea winds cut like a razor and made the rain slap your face like a scorned woman. Sometimes practice was exhilarating. Fifty guys lined up in perfect rows practicing form-fit tackling in the pouring rain, obeying my every command shouted loud enough to be heard above wind and the raindrops thumping the helmets. On those nights I felt like Denzel Washington in *Remember the Titans*, a commander who roamed the field like a football god orchestrating greatness. Other practices were much more disappointing, such as when we had to cancel practice because not enough players decided to show up. Those nights I felt more like Sparky Woods, the hapless former coach of my beloved University of South Carolina, a program that has achieved unenviable mediocrity in its one hundred plus years of football. Again, paradox.

Turkey is a long way from Tuscaloosa. Located between the Black and Mediterranean seas, Turkey is a gateway country between Europe and Asia and is roughly 6,000 miles from the University of Alabama, the premier collegiate football program in the United States. But if you consider their respective brands of American football, Turkey might as well be in outer space. In Tuscaloosa, more than 100,000 fans fill Bryant-Denny Stadium to watch some of the finest college football our nation has to offer. A football Saturday in the South offers pomp and pageantry, beer and brawn, cheerleaders and chicken, touchdowns, defense, and Lee Corso in an elephant head. In Turkey, our team once played in a sheep pasture, where the only spectators were military police officers surrounding the field with M-16 rifles and the displaced sheep. A football Saturday in the Turkish Republic offers cigarettes and sheep dung, turnovers and traffic, chants and chai, missed tackles, missed calls, and an old lady in a headscarf. Toto, we're not in SEC country anymore.

I never would have expected to find American football in the heart of the old Ottoman Empire. It seems out of place, like if the University of Miami somehow got invited to play in the Ivy League. After all, the United States is not exactly the most well-liked nation in this part of the world. For Turks, the word *football* always refers to soccer, hence the necessity of the qualifier *American*. Further, Turkey is 99.9 percent Muslim and we do not normally associate the Five Pillars of Islam with a five-man rush.

Yet there I was less than 24 hours after stepping off the plane to a new life in Istanbul, coaching the Stallions. Roaming that soccer field overlooking the Black Sea I barked out instructions about how to block and tackle in a language half the team did not understand. They responded in a language I did not understand, which was one of many signs that we had a thousand different life experiences. We grew up with different cultural norms, political systems, religions,

11

family structures, sports, foods, and ideas about how the world works. And, yet, in our differences, joy abounded on that football field. Such is the beauty of sport. It is transcultural and translingual. It matters not if one speaks Turkish, English, Kurmanji, or Quenya, the thud of shoulder pads colliding elicits the same neanderthal-like grunt from men of all ages and cultures. A well-timed smack to the numbers knows no national borders and needs no defined grammatical structure to be appreciated. So we stood there at the end of that first practice with all our differences as obvious as a quarterback sneak on fourth-and-inches and no one cared a bit. We shared a field and a football and a common goal. We wanted to win football games—the team had not won a game in two years—and have fun doing it.

The Stallions were founded by students from several Istanbul universities, but functioned as part of the Koç University Sports Club. The club fielded two American football squads, a university team made up solely of Koç students and a professional team comprised of mostly university students and recent graduates from all around Istanbul, though none of the "professional" players were actually paid. The university played under the nickname Rams—which is the meaning of the Turkish word *koç*—while the Stallions were the professional team. Until 2010 both Koç and Yıldız Technical Universities fielded separate professional squads. But seeing an opportunity to form a stronger team together, the two clubs merged into the team that I coached. As a nod to each nickname our team's rallying motto became "*Hit like a Ram, Run like a Stallion, Win like a Champion.*" In the summer of 2013 the merger agreement was dissolved and the varying factions went their separate ways.

The teams practiced and played home games on the university's campus tucked away in the Belgrade Forest in Istanbul's northern district of Sarıyer. The university, founded in 1993 by the tycoon Koç family, is a leading private university in Turkey and an educational haven for the wealthy and ambitious. The Henry Ford Building on campus hints at the Koç family's business dynasty, one that operates some of the most profitable and prestigious companies in Turkey, including Ford automobile dealerships.

Turkey, home to seventy-some-odd million people, is located at the very western edge of the ancient Silk Road trading route. This strategic location between Europe and Asia has shaped much of its cultural identity and cast a constant state of cultural tension upon its citizenry. Turkey is where East meets West, ancient meets modern, and secular meets dogmatically religious. These tensions have contributed to something of an identity crisis among Turks; an identity crisis that very well may have put American football on the tee in Turkey.

Istanbul is Turkey's largest and most influential city. As the former seat of the Roman, Byzantine, and Ottoman Empires, Istanbul is the historical heart of Turkey. On the drive from the airport you can see city walls a thousand years older than the United States of America. The city's architecture provides a helpful index of the various empires that have ruled the city. Most notable are the dueling houses of worship, the Byzantine Hagia Sophia Church and the Ottoman Sultanahmet Mosque that face one another across a pedestrian courtyard. The city also serves as the country's economic engine. As jobs and industry disappear from small towns and as villages move away from their agrarian roots, Turks are forced migrate to Istanbul for *ekmek parası*, or bread money. Some younger Turks welcome this trend as an opportunity to shake the dust off their low-top Converses at their tired hometowns and move to the fast lights of Taksim Square and *Istiklal Caddesi*, the most famous street in Turkey. For others, however, the drain from villages to Istanbul is a slow and painful death to a once-treasured way of life.

Istanbul is the population hub of Turkey with over a quarter of its residents residing in the world's only transcontinental city. It is overwhelmingly massive. I vividly remember looking out of the airplane's window as we descended into the city for the first time, flabbergasted by the amount of concrete I saw in every direction. From above, apartment buildings looked like a million drab colored matchboxes stacked on top of one another. It appeared as if at any moment a strong wind—or worse, the big earthquake every Turk fears—could flick them all away.

The official population is listed as twelve million, but when one accounts for new arrivals, foreigners, and illegal workers eighteen million seems to be the more accepted estimate. One best senses the massiveness of the city while in transit. Fish analogies are cliche, but sardines and salmon do come to mind on packed minibuses and metro station corridors. I am convinced congested highway traffic and the ensuing road rage is responsible for as many Istanbulite heart attacks as the copious amounts of oil consumed at Turkish tables. The frustration is tangible.

Traffic is so horrendous, urban legend has it that the local government once hired a Japanese firm to study the city's traffic flow —or lack thereof—and come up with a solution. After months of study the firm replied, "We have no idea how your traffic works as it is, but whatever you do, do not try to fix it because you may never get it working again." At three in the morning I can drive to a friend's house in fifteen minutes. At mid-afternoon the same drive takes an hour. At rush hour, I refuse to look at the clock and resign myself to enjoying a *simit*, a ring-shaped piece of bread bought from the snack vendor walking between the lanes of halted traffic.

Posted traffic rules in Turkey are mostly decorations. The signs look nice and official, but nobody obeys them. Contrary to first impression, Istanbul traffic is not chaotic. Unwritten rules exist, six of which I have discerned:

Rule #1: The rock, paper, scissors rule, or *the bus, van, taxi* rule. Bus beats van because it is bigger and bigger vehicle usually wins (Rule 1A). Van beats taxi (see Rule 1A), but taxi beats bus because taxi drivers are crazier than bus drivers and so Rule 1A does not apply in this case.

Rule #2: The one finger rule. You can do anything you want—cut someone off, step out in the middle of traffic, make an illegal U-turn, pickpocket a grandmother—as long as you gesture with your index finger like you are saying "just one second." At this gesture you immediately get *carte blanche* immunity for whatever you do next and I've found it to be quite useful.

Rule #3: The if you miss your exit, just back up rule. This one's pretty self-explanatory. If you miss your exit you don't just wait to the next exit and turn around as there likely will not be a next exit and, even if there is, you will not be able to turn around. Instead, you stop, put on your flashers, and back up on the highway until you can make your turn. I've seen countless drivers execute this move and I've done it once or twice while driving around a group of Americans just to see their reactions and snicker to myself. This maneuver is a timesaver and provides a little extra adrenaline (or anxiety) to all in the vehicle.

Rule #4: The if there is empty space, take it rule. This is the rule that causes most of the traffic congestion. There is no concept of waiting your turn in a line here. If there is space in front of you, you are allowed to take it. Emergency lanes or any other paved surface not previously occupied by a vehicle are fair game to drive in, even if it means causing all traffic to stop 100 meters ahead when vehicles will have to merge back into the normal lanes. This rule is also in play at fast food counters, ATMs, and lines at government offices, so developing wide elbows and losing my Southern manners were necessary adjustments.

Rule #5: The horn rule. When all else fails—there is no emergency lane to drive in and you can't back up and even the *just one second* finger does not work—lay on the horn. Repeatedly. It has to help, right?

Rule #6: The if you need it you can buy it rule. If you need something while you are stuck in traffic, odds are you can buy it from a guy in the middle of the highway. Hungry? Help yourself to an overpriced banana or a cardboard-tasting waffle. Thirsty? He's got water. Dead cell phone? Choose from an assortment of chargers. You can also buy flowers, bread, bubble machines, or a toy bow-and-arrow set. And let's be honest, who among us hasn't been stuck in traffic and thought, "*you know what I could really go for... a bow and arrow!"*

If you are confused as to why grown men would stand in the center lanes of a major highway and sell toy bow-and-arrow sets there are two things you need to know about Turkish culture. First, it appears that many Turkish children are not disciplined until they serve their mandatory military service. Thus, bribery for good behavior starts early; chocolate for babies and toys for children in traffic. Second, you should know that Turks and Native Americans are cousins, or so I've been told a hundred times since moving here. As the story goes, both groups originated from Mongolia. The Turks traveled west and began a series of military excursions into what is now Turkey, retreating back to the north each time, before realizing it was really cold in the north land and deciding to conquer the land above the Mediterranean and relocate there. Native Americans, however, traveled east across the Bering Strait and settled in America. Thus, they are cousins, allegedly. In Istanbul I've seen a full head-dressed Native American band playing and selling CDs by the sea. And one neighborhood pizza maker, knowing my wife has some Cherokee blood in her, would do an "Indian call" every time he saw her on the street. A Turkish cowboy and Indian television series, set in what looks like the American West, but with Turkish cowboys and Indians speaking Turkish, also airs on Turkish television. And though this has nothing to do with Native Americans, but loosely with cowboy television shows, I feel it is worth mentioning that *Dallas* was a huge television hit in the 1980s in Turkey, so much that some friends still tell me about it. There were very few television channels at that time and, for some reason, one of them showed *Dallas*. I cannot express the surprise I felt when a very devout Muslim shopkeeper in my neighborhood inquired as to who shot J.R.

Istanbul is also Turkey's cultural capital, if not its political one. Traditional Turkish culture is preserved outside of Istanbul, across the country in villages and small towns with handmade crafts, traditional food, and folk dances. But current culture—music, movies, fashion, commerce, and political ideas—flows from Istanbul. What begins in the city eventually makes it to the village, which is precisely how our team ended up playing American football in that sheep pasture surrounded by military police.

American football in Turkey began on the campus of Boğaziçi University, on the European side of Istanbul, in 1987 when a group of curious students played a pick-up game against United States navy men. With no background or frame of reference for the sport, the Boğaziçi students learned the rules as the game went along (sometimes I think today's referees are still learning the rules as the games go along). The students formed a club and news spread to other universities in Istanbul and Ankara, the nation's capital. By 1993 five universities fielded club teams, *sans* equipment. The Boğaziçi Elephants and the Istanbul Pistoflar played the first game between two Turkish teams at the annual Boğaziçi University Sports Fest, an event that hosts students from all over Turkey and Europe each spring to compete in a wide range of sports from soccer to basketball to ultimate frisbee. Realizing that the Elephant, though original, was a slightly ridiculous nickname, Boğaziçi, with a tip of the fez to their Ottoman heritage, soon changed their nickname to the Sultans.

For the next two years teams played a series of tournaments, continuing to rough it without equipment, but still tackling. Like their professional sports counterparts in the United States, the fledgling league was not immune to a stoppage in play. The 1997-98 campaign was cancelled due to a misunderstanding among teams about procedures and rules, though Boğaziçi won a symbolic championship game against the Middle East Technical University Falcons.

Equipment slowly began to trickle into Turkey. Interested Americans donated some equipment, while universities and players scrounged up enough money to purchase more. The 2001-02 season was the first with protective gear. Boğaziçi, always ahead of the curve, won the first game played with full equipment, defeating the Bilkent Judges 34-0.

As the sport developed so did its organization. Two leagues

emerged in 2003-04. The easternmost teams, usually from Ankara, played in the *Amerikan Futbol Kurulu* (AFK), while teams from the west played in the stronger *Ulusal Amerikan Futbol Ligi* (UAFL). In 2005 the government's sports ministry took over the sport, placing American football under the Turkish Baseball and Softball Federation, and thus the Turkish American Football League was born. The first TAFL Championship was played in Istanbul's İnönü Stadium, home to the popular soccer club, Beşiktaş, on live television. Predictably, the Sultans won the championship, defeating Izmir's Ege Dolphins 30-8.

The TAFL expanded to 18 teams in 2006 and further expanded in 2009, creating a two-division professional league and a university league. Today close to fifty teams compete across all leagues and divisions, most all of which have English nicknames, a nod to the sport's American roots and the general Westward gaze of urban Turks who play the game. Turkish American football, like many new cultural phenomena, was born in Istanbul but has spread to cities such as Ankara, Izmir, Mersin, Konya, and even Sakarya, home of the sheep field.

Unlike Turkish children I had the opportunity to watch and play American football from an early age. I grew up with the game, playing in recreation and school leagues and attending games at the University of South Carolina. After playing quarterback in high school I made it my goal to be a schoolteacher so that I could coach high school football and basketball, the sports I coached at local high schools while attending university. Sports were what I knew and loved.

Through a series of events I never taught school but worked in collegiate athletic administration for a few years before moving to North Carolina to attend graduate school. There, I met Coach Jay who first introduced me to the Stallions opportunity. Jay had been in contact with an American businessman in Istanbul named Zane, whose company sponsored the team as a community development project. Zane had agreed to bring him over as a coach and so over coffee one night I asked Jay if he thought that the team might want two coaches and, if so, I was interested. After some communication, Zane worked it out for both of our families to move to Turkey to coach the Stallions.

Zane is better known as Baba Zane with the football players. *Baba* means father and that is appropriate because Zane became a father figure for many of the players. One evening while working out at a local gym, Zane was approached by a young man named Seyfo, then one of the leaders of the Stallions and the most powerful running back in Turkey. A quick glance at their biceps would reveal that both men loved lifting weights and they must have felt some solidarity in the bench press in a gym filled with covered girls on the elliptical machines and overweight men walking on treadmills. Seyfo remarked to Zane, "you are American, you should come coach our football team." Zane, being kind and eager to make local friends, replied that he would be glad to entertain the idea. A few days later, thinking he was going to meet with the team leaders to discuss the possibility, he walked into a room with the entire team and was promptly introduced as the team's new coach. Not one to disappoint a room full of boisterous university students, he acquiesced.

Baba Zane traveled a lot for work and knew that he did not have the time to be the permanent head coach. But the team was too fun to walk away from completely so he used his American connections to help provide the team with coaches, equipment, and some funding for away game road trips. And so he settled into the *Baba* role, loving the players like a father, giving wise counsel, and helping them achieve their goals. A fun side note on Zane. He is also the intellectual equivalent of Ray Lewis, which is to say that he is really stinking smart. As such he knew multiple languages from his time working in various countries. Because he traveled often and knew English, Farsi, Turkish, and some Russian, the joke on the team was that he was a CIA agent, a common assumption of foreigners by many Turks. With a touch of comedic timing, it just so happened that Zane took a new job and moved back to the United States shortly after Osama Bin Laden was killed in the spring of 2011, a detail that was not lost on our players who thought it more than coincidence. Translating Zane's farewell speech to the team, Berk translated "I'm leaving my current company to take a new job in America" as "I'm leaving the CIA to take a new job in America."

We all laughed. And most of us knew that it was simply a joke.

ÇAY BREAK

I paid a man to bathe me.

It's not as bad as it seems, though. I promise.

After eighteen months of refusal I relented and visited a hamam, *or Turkish Bath. It was for a special occasion—a friend was moving back to America—so seven of us guys loaded up and drove to the Asian side of Istanbul for the bubbly good time, as if going to a separate continent made it acceptable to be bathed by another man.*

"What is a hamam?," you might ask. Here's the skinny.

Upon entering the bathhouse we were shown a room where you leave all your stuff. And by all your stuff I mean all of it. Even the skivvies. You wrap a towel resembling a tablecloth around you and head to the bath.

All's good so far.

Once in the bath area we sat and poured water on ourselves. The room was hot and the room is steamy, an unfortunate choice of words when you are sitting around with other men, but temperately accurate nonetheless. It felt like a sauna, except the sauna was much hotter. After the sauna we cooled down by pouring some more water on ourselves, while sitting around and chatting.

All's still good.

At this point what I thought was another patron walked into our little side room. I thought to myself, why wouldn't I want to get a little Turkish speaking practice in while wearing nothing but picnic plaid?, *so I started to chat with him. I realized he was not just another patron when he grabbed my friend's head and slapped him on the back like a jockey to a derby horse. He was the professional bather. He was burly, hairy, and had hands strong enough to choke a man without so much as a grimace. He wore a mitten that felt like a cross between sandpaper and an SOS pad and used it to scrub off all the dead skin.*

Things just got interesting.

After the scrubbing comes the massaging. One by one we were led to a large, heated marble slab in the middle of the room. The tablecloth became a loincloth as the attendant rearranged it for optimal massage positioning, or something like that. I was lathered, battered, massaged, smacked, cracked, and doused with water colder than Lambeau Field.

The massage was one part "This feels really awkward", *one part* "This feels really relaxing", *one part* "This kind of hurts", *one part* "This kind of tickles", *and all parts awesome.*

The last part of the experience is going back to your little room to lie on the bed and rest for a while. This moment of quiet and relaxing reflection allows one to contemplate the deeper questions of life, like What is my purpose on earth?, What is the role of faith in society?, *and* Why did I just pay a man to bathe me? *It is in this moment that I'm inclined to agree with a friend who describes having gone to the hamam as both the cleanest you will ever feel… and the dirtiest.*

3

FIRST DOWN AND MILES TO GO

When Mustafa Kemal resurrected the Turkish state from the rubble left by the Ottoman Sultanate and the plans to partition the land by Western powers at the end of World War I, he established the modern Republic of Turkey by sheer imposition of his will. With the word of his voice and the ink of his pen, he abolished the Ottoman Empire, sending both the Sultan and Islamic Caliph into exile, heads firmly tucked beneath their tails. Seeing a nation of twelve million Anatolians, mostly villagers, mostly Muslim, living a mostly eastern and un-modern lifestyle, Kemal's dream was to drag Turkey into modern Western civilization, but not with kicking and screaming. No, he silenced anyone who opposed his program of civilizing—Europeanizing—the Turks, and kicking and screaming opposition was punishable by death. So he outlawed the fez, a traditional Ottoman hat chock with Islamic symbolism, and mandated men wear hats with bills, like any self-respecting European. He also outlawed the head scarf for women and gave them the right to vote to boot. He replaced the Arabic script with a Latin one and made education a cardinal virtue for the young nation.

A son of the Enlightenment—he read Voltaire and Rousseau in French—Kemal directed that science and reason were to be the guiding lights for this nation transformed. He mandated that Western dress be the norm, the call to Muslim prayer to be chanted in Turkish rather than Arabic—though later repealed—and the head of each family to choose a surname for his family. Up to that point there was no need for surnames, as Turkey was mostly a collection of villages where everybody knew the one Muhammad who resided there. Kemal chose Atatürk, meaning "father of the Turks" as his surname and forbid anyone else take it.

Atatürk's goal was to move Turkey westward, into Europe, and to make it a democratic country, a fish far out of the normal Central Asian political water. The irony is that Atatürk could not transform Turkey into a modern, Western, democratic state through democratic means. The masses rallied to him as their savior from Western powers that intended to give away their land to Greece, Italy, France, and others in the wake of World War I. But like most people, Turks did not want to give up everything from their past. Many residents were against some of Atatürk's more radical ideas, particularly the ones dealing with religion. So Atatürk was forced to impose his modernization project on Turkey by sheer power, which was sometimes displayed by sword or noose. He silenced his critics and killed his opponents. And in so doing he won the admiration of the Turkish people as a strong and valiant leader.

Today, in every town stands a statue of Atatürk, in every office a portrait. It is against the law to "curse Atatürk's memory." If he ever slept at a house, it has most likely been converted into a museum called an Atatürk House. Hundreds of such houses are scattered across the country. On November 10th, the anniversary of his death, at the precise time of his last breath, 9:10 a.m., the nation comes to a screeching halt. Literally. For one solid minute of memorial, highway traffic stops as taxi drivers stand at attention, sirens blare, and everyone solemnly remembers their hero. The one possible exception is that one minibus driver who forgets what day it is, though he will suddenly slam on brakes as soon as he realizes what is happening.

Every neighborhood has one of these drivers.

Atatürk's modernization project has largely succeeded, at least on the surface. An identity crisis remains, a subject treated elsewhere in this book, but the modernization of Turkey cannot go unnoticed. Skyscrapers dominate much of Istanbul's cityscape; Europe is heavily invested in Turkey's economy; and Turks have eclipsed educational heights unimagined for their ancestors just a few generations ago, with many of Turkey's brightest earning Ph.D's in London and New York and around the world. Turks work for international banks and corporations both in Turkey and abroad. Some hold very prominent positions, such as Muhtar Kent, the current chairman and CEO of the Coca-Cola Company. The nation has become a major player on the geopolitical stage, particularly as a Middle East power broker. Technology has advanced to the farthest corner of the country, so much so that high in the Kaçkar mountains, I have a friend who religiously follows the New Orleans Saints via satellite television and high-speed internet from his wooden village home.

Though Turkey's advance into modernism and into the Western conscious has been rapid, it is not yet complete. There are too many mosques, too many animistic superstitions, too much village mentality, and, frankly, too much belief in God to say Turkey is completely at home in modernism or Westernism. Still, the Atatürkian footprints of modernity cannot be ignored. The country is too politically stable, economically profitable, culturally progressive, and nationally democratic to lump it in wholesale with other Middle Eastern and Central Asian states. The value of this quest of modernity and Western acceptance is best left for another discussion. For now, it suffices to point to the one man who willed Turkey to where it is today, a successful and increasingly significant global nation. Mustafa Kemal Atatürk was a cultural architect before hipsters made such nomenclature cool and his fingerprints—not to mention his portrait—are found in every corner and cranny of the country and its culture.

Unlike Atatürk's national program, the introduction of American football into Turkish sport culture has been less than revolutionary. Atatürk may have imported swaths of European culture by the force of his will and personality, but American football has slogged along like Istanbul's famous winter fog. Introduced in 1987 by American servicemen, the sport remains mostly unknown and without interest nearly three decades later. Equipment is still hard to come by, as is decent officiating. A government federation runs the university and professional leagues, but it runs them rather less well than a horse would ride another horse, to paraphrase the Black Adder. Teams only play an average of six games per season, a season that lasts from September to June. Attendance is low, sponsorship money lower, and the absence of a bona fide youth league means that the composite skill level has not increased proportionally to the sport's three decades in Turkey.

But *yavaş yavaş*—"slowly, slowly"—American football is making progress. It is plodding and slogging progress, kind of like a Big Ten offense, but it is progress. The number of teams and players is increasing. The sport's marketing is improving, most notably a program dedicated to American football on satellite television. And on the field, the passing game—long the Turkish game's kryptonite —is even making productive strides. Still, as a *New York Times* headline read several years ago, for American football in Turkey it is "First Down and Miles to Go."

The Stallions' progression over the past decade provides a microcosm of the progression of American football in Turkey. In the beginning, friends simply gathered to start playing even without equipment. As they recruited friends to play, they formed a club and travelled to Mersin for the club's first game ever. Since the team only had fifteen sets of equipment, they only took fifteen players. However, when they arrived in Mersin, the Crows (North Cyprus) no-showed the game. Fifteen players traveled fifteen hours for a false start, a common theme in the evolution of American football in Turkey. In their first real game, you know, one where the other team actually showed up, the Stallions suffered a crushing 120 0 defeat. It did not get much better from there as they finished the season winless. In their second season, the Stallions won two games, downing Sakarya and Yeditepe. The Yeditepe win, however, was a forfeit because their coach took his team off the field after a fight broke out when an opposing player spoke curse words about a Stallions player's mother.

The first Stallions coach, a Turk from Ankara, was dismissed after two games, in part because he spent the fourth quarter of one game on his cell phone. Berkay took over coaching duties at that point until Seyfo met Baba Zane that night in the fitness center. Zane worked some connections to bring an American to coach the team, a high-energy, no-nonsense guy named Tim. The team lost Coach Tim's first game to Istanbul Technical University (ITU) after two interceptions derailed their efforts. The squad lost fifteen players after that game. Some players did not want to play for an American. Others, most likely, did not want to play for someone who enforced team discipline. Others simply had to attend to work or military obligations. Yet, for those who stayed, Coach Tim became an older brother figure, though he was about the same age as some of the players. He ran a high-discipline system and focused on both the fundamentals of the game and the fundamentals of the team's character. Seyfo, who spent nearly every day with Tim for a season of life, gushes when he talks about his friend. According to Seyfo, a team leader, Coach Tim gave the team its mentality and was a guy who could change people. He helped players on and off the field, encouraging players to be good students, to be good people, and to believe in God, Seyfo said. He wanted the Stallions to be better people, not just better football players. Tim's involvement with the team represents a larger American influence on the game in Turkey. Introduced by Americans, the game has been significantly influenced by Americans who have provided instructional clinics and coaching services for Turkish clubs.

The wins never did pile up for the Stallions. One player summed their situation up well, saying, "we lost a lot of games, but we loved each other." In 2009, as teams started looking more for a competitive edge, ITU proposed a merger between the two teams. However, as it became apparent that they just wanted to use the merger as a way to steal the Stallions best players, the deal was rejected. Next, Koç University proposed a merger. Though doubt existed as to whether the Stallions could get along with the rich, private school Koç students, the team leaders decided it would be a beneficial transaction. Tactically, Koç had a plethora of quality skill position players while the Stallions had a stable of well-fed linemen. Logistically, Koç had a field that could be used rent-free while the Stallions had equipment and coaches. The merger helped both teams.

Shortly after the merger, in spring of 2010, the new Koç Stallions faced ITU in the final regular season game. Balıkçı, a mammoth defensive lineman, intercepted an errant ITU pass to score the winning touchdown, but a roughing the passer penalty denied the team its only win of the season. Still, the team took confidence from the near-victory into the playout game against the Crows. The team flew to North Cyprus for the game and this time the Crows showed up. Mirroring the soccer system, the winner would stay in the first division and the loser would be relegated to the second division. Trailing by a touchdown, Onur beat the corner deep by twenty yards. Wide open with nothing but grass between him and victory, the ball bounced off his hands like a living metaphor for the Stallions. So close, but so far. Almost, but not yet. They lost the game and were relegated to the second division where they still play to this day.

Coach Jay and I took the coaching reigns later in 2010. After the merger the Stallions squad was much stronger, combining skill position players with linemen in a way the team had never had before. We also had four "imports" on our team, four Americans living in Istanbul for a semester as part of a cultural exchange program. We rolled off an undefeated regular season, a feat that sounds more impressive when you leave out the part about the season only being five games. Still, it was five games more than the team had won in a while. As second division champions we advanced to the playout game with a chance to earn a spot back in the first division. In true Turkish fashion, this game was continuously postponed for one reason or another. I suspect that our opponent from Ankara knew we had several stud imports that they could not handle and kept making excuses for why they could not play until mid-June, a good three weeks after the Americans' exchange program finished and they flew back to the United States.

Down a few starters, including our quarterback, Coach Jay and I decided to suit up for this game. I had not played competitive football in about ten years, not since I left in the second quarter of the second game of my senior season in high school with an ACL injury. Playing in this game gave me the chance to relive my high school glory days, if being an average-at-best quarterback on an average small high school team qualifies as glory in any respect of the word. Playing in this game also made it possible to credibly tell my grandchildren that I played professional football in Europe (technically, I played the game in Ankara, which is in Asia, but we practiced on and were based from the European side of Istanbul, so I'm counting it). I felt confident in practice and was looking forward to faking an inside isolation and scooting around the corner and down the sidelines for a touchdown. Unfortunately, the opposing team's defensive ends were a little faster than the ones I practiced against and I could not reach the outside. Two interceptions later and my daydreams of football glory were sufficiently sacked. Still, we had a chance to win at the end. We put Coach Jay at wide receiver, a move I stupidly did not make earlier in the game, and we advanced the ball inside the red zone, but ran out of time on the 18-yard line.

And just like that, our season fizzled into summer vacations. We walked off the field, stunned that we lost. I walked off the field angry. I was angry at my two interceptions, one of which was a horrendous attempt to throw across my body of which I knew better than to attempt. I was angry that our best receiver got kicked out of the game because he could not control his temper. I was angry that the receivers left in the game could not remember how to run the arrow deep route, forcing me to try to make a play by throwing across my body. I was angry that for a month leading up to our most important game of the season we never had our entire team all together at one practice session. A season later, we lost the season opener, but ran the table the rest of the regular season. Unfortunately, we dropped the

playout game again, this time in Eskişehir. I left this game angry as
well, this time at the two veteran players who pitched a sideline
tantrum because they were suspended for missing a month's worth of
practices.

Anger is a heat-of-the-moment emotion and, thankfully, it faded
quickly. The frustration, however, does not go quite so easily.
Frustration is a good word to describe American football in Turkey.
The unrealized potential, the unmet promise, leaves one frustrated
that the sport is left to limp along like an old quarterback with a
nagging knee injury. Like my two Stallions seasons, the sport in
Turkey has shown flashes of promise. Turkey has two growing
leagues, a nationally televised studio program, a cult of devoted young
fans, expert coaches willing to move to Turkey, and outlets for
international competition. Yet, like my two Stallions seasons that
ended in bickering defeat, American football in Turkey keeps getting
sacked for a loss. The talent level is not significantly improving, fan
(that is, potential customer) interest remains low, and the leagues are
run with the stereotypical efficiency of the Department of Motor
Vehicles. But why? What are the root problems? Or, in offensive line
terms, who missed their assignment that led to the quarterback sack?

In this case, the *Turkish Baseball, Softball, Protective Football, and
Rugby Federation* is like the right tackle who is just a little too fat and
slow to reach the five-technique. This six-man cabal is responsible for
oversight and implementation of the minority sports listed in its title.
But those who run the federation have little invested in the success of
American football. In the view of some players, the Federation does
not seem to care particularly if the sport succeeds or fails in Turkey,
they just want to be in position to profit from the sport if it ever does
take off. But because of a lack of assertive leadership in favor of
football's growth, the sport is currently positioned to never take off.
Some even question the Federation's financial stewardship. Rugby is
reported to receive a more favorable status—and thus more focused
energy and funding—because it is an Olympic sport that represents a
greater probability of profitability. American football insiders feel as
if they are continually getting sacked by their own team, left without

the resources and structures to succeed.

The Federation's lack of commitment to the game's success is on full display in the two duties that it is directly responsible for: scheduling and officiating. There is no regularly scheduled and set American football season in Turkey. Teams start training in September and usually finish the season in early June, making for a nine-month season. In that span, a team will likely play six games at the most. In 2010-11, the Koç University team played a whopping three games. In my second season we opened the season in December, had a bye in March, and played our next league game in April. Granted, Turkish culture is less structured than American culture and I have learned to accept loose plans. But the lack of an identified season with games played in regular intervals has stymied opportunities to gain fan interest because no one—players, coaches, officials, much less fans—knows when a game will be played from week to week. Also, without an identified, structured season it is difficult to gather all players on a team for practice regularly. Most players are either studying or working and cannot commit to attending every practice for nine months. Further, who wants to practice football in the cold mid-January rain when the next scheduled game is in March? So a team never has a chance to bond and build momentum together, diminishing the quality of football on the field.

A regular eight-week season, plus playoffs, would be the ideal scenario. Teams would be able to play enough games to make the season worth it and everyone would know that there would be a game every week. Why can this not happen? Because there are not enough referees to officiate this many games on one weekend. Why? Because the Federation's effort to recruit, train, and compensate a sufficient number of officials has been equivalent to Tiger Woods's effort at fidelity.

I watched a university league game with Umut, the head official in Istanbul and a former player who makes his living as a lawyer. He told me the 2013 season was almost cancelled when he and his colleagues threatened not to officiate if they were not paid several years' worth of unpaid wages. The officials and the Federation reached an agreement when the Federation paid the officials for the 2011 season and for two 2013 games. The 2012 season wages remain unpaid. Umut also told me that there are no efforts to stock new officials outside of him recruiting those within his social network. As we stood on the sidelines he pointed to the referees officiating the game and remarked how they were all his friends and one was his brother. He annually provides a single training clinic at the beginning of each season, but not all officials attend as they are not required to do so. The Federation provides no other training and does not issue any sort of officiating license. In addition to the insufficient numbers of referees, the quality of officiating is also damaging to the health and prospective growth of the game, a topic that will be treated elsewhere in this book. In our conversation, Umut playfully boasted that he is the best official in Turkey. Having witnessed most of the others, I agree. He knows the game and is fair. However, in the same sentence he also admitted that he is not great, a statement that I also co-sign because he is the official who ejected me from a game for arguing what was in my estimation an obviously missed call.

Though the progress of American football is slow and choppy in Turkey, the strength and beauty of the sport here is found in the very same place that Umut finds his fellow officials: the social network. To this concept we now turn.

4

ÇEVRE

Çevre is an important Turkish word, referring to one's circle of relationships. The center of one's *çevre* is his family, but it extends out to neighbors, friends, work relationships, and shopkeepers. *Çevre* is important because relationships are important. Turks value the communal over the individual, which means concepts such as honor and shame are prevalent in Turkish thinking. In the opening chapter I wrote that Turkey has both glory and grunge. The glory of *çevre* is that Turks are not individualistic, but rely on one another, live in community, and experience life in relationship with others. Time spent over tea with a friend is more important than the next task to be done on a to-do list. Honoring one another with terms of affection or respect is another glory of the *çevre*. But taken to its extreme, *çevre* is filled with grunge. In recent years Turkey has seen a resurgence in honor killings, murders for the sake of protecting the family's honor.

In 2010, a sixteen-year-old girl was buried alive in her family's garden in Kahta, covered with concrete, because she brought shame on her family by talking to boys. In 2011, a nineteen-year-old woman was murdered in Mersin by her brother for, as a news report cited, "besmirching the family's honor." She was stabbed 40 times. In 2012, a woman in southwestern Turkey was repeatedly sexually assaulted by her husband's uncle while her husband was out of town working. The uncle took naked photographs of the woman and used the photographic evidence of her "unfaithfulness" to control her. Even though she was the victim of rape, had he shown the photographs to others, she would have been seen as the one who besmirched the honor of the family and her children would have been insulted. The abuse began when the uncle broke into her house to rape her and threaten to kill her children if she did not submit quietly. Eight months later, when she heard him coming to rape her again, she grabbed a gun and shot him in the crotch. She then proceeded to cut his head off and march down to the town square, carrying the uncle's head by his hair to present it to a group of men. "Do not talk behind my back, do not play with my honor. This is the head of the man who played with my honor," she bellowed before tossing the head to the ground. She was arrested without trouble, simply declaring that she saved her honor and that her kids would be known as the children of the woman who saved her honor.

Honor killings are rare, but their existence in Turkey illustrates the collective nature of relationships in Turkey. One's sins—real or perceived—are not simply one's own. They shame the entire community, the *çevre*. Likewise, one's accomplishments bring honor on the entire group, which explains great national and city pride when one of their own does well in public.

To be accepted by someone is to be welcomed by their *çevre* as well. Upon arriving in Istanbul I was quickly assimilated into the Stallions' *çevre*. Onur, the team president and a wide receiver, became my first friend in Turkey and when you move to a foreign country you need friends. I am grateful for how he welcomed us and helped us ease into life in Turkey. He took the responsibility to incorporate Coach Jay and me into the life of the team and made sure we were in the team *çevre* by introducing us to people and inviting us out. Part of Onur's shtick is to play the part of Mr. Turkish Tradition, jokingly making sure that all foreigners associated with the team experience all that traditional Turkish culture has to offer, most notably the tradition of greeting each other with a kiss. He appreciates the old Turkish traditions, particularly when it comes to food and drink and holidays, but he also likes to make up his own. For instance, when out in the city together, he will insist the group pose for what he calls a traditional photo, where everyone crouches and gazes wistfully into the distance in different directions. Another Onur tradition is making the American coaches eat *kokoreç*, a sheep intestines sandwich, when visiting the tourist sites. And though I have a tradition of not eating the bowels of any caprinae, I succumbed and ate because, well, it is tradition. Like any good president of anything, he has a knack for getting whatever he wants and he usually gets it by carrying on the Turkish tradition of talking. He might sweet-talk you or he might make you feel foolish or he might just talk you into submission with his loquaciousness, but he will get what he wants. I've seen him talk Federation officials into allowing unlicensed players to play. When he was serving his compulsory military duty he talked his way into Facebook access and watching the Super Bowl, privileges that are normally forbidden. His buttery speech is one of the reasons he made such a good team president.

My favorite of Onur's Turkish traditions is drinking hot drinks with friends while telling jokes and stories. But rather than frequenting the local tea house, we often went to Starbucks, which highlights the shifting culture of many young Istanbul Turks. They hold tightly to friendships and passing time chatting and drinking together because relationships are so important. But now they gather at a western chain coffee shop, replacing the customary black tea with lattes, mochas, and coffees. Istanbul alone is home to more than eighty Starbucks stores, my favorite being located in Bebek, an old money neighborhood near the Bosphorus Strait on the European side of the city. This particular location has patio seating right on the water, putting every drive-through Starbucks in shopping centers across America to open shame.

One night soon after arriving in Istanbul, Onur picked me up and drove me to the Bebek Starbucks to meet some other team leaders. As it turned out to be the usual case, Onur's brother Reha was along for the evening. Reha had played football for a little while, but a shoulder injury forced an early retirement. I nicknamed Reha "The Professor" because he is wickedly smart, particularly when it comes to history, and has an ability to explain Ottoman history like a seasoned academic.

Onur and Reha first became exposed to American football through a Dan Marino video game when they were growing up. Plenty of soccer video games could be found in Turkey at the time, but this was the first American football game. At this time they could only get news of American football, but no games. Then, Fox Sports started showing one game per week, always an NFC game, which disappointed Reha as he became a huge New England Patriots fan through Playstation and computer video games. Their cousin, Emre, had befriended a guy on the Yıldız Technical University team and started attending the training camp. Emre summoned Onur and Reha to the camp, telling them "you are always playing football on the computer, come play the real game." Reha, deploying for military service, was unable to go, but Onur joined the team.

Before he started going by President Onur, he earned the nickname "fire toes" because of his red cleats. Nicknames were used because the team did not know each other's names at first. Onur worked his way to team president by demonstrating toughness, trustworthiness, and a little traditional political savvy. He fractured his leg in an Oklahoma drill once, but did not let it slow him down. He drove home on it that night and continued practicing with the team. The president at that time started trusting him with the money —players would chip in what they could to help pay for the field rental. Eventually, he became president of the club and wielded considerable influence on the team, even if he was not a breakout player.

Berkay, one of the founders of the team, also met us at Starbucks that night. Berkay was an imposing figure at first. Tall and big with dark hair and olive skin, he dressed nice and wasn't shy about talking or spending money. I nicknamed him the Godfather since he came across much like what I imagined a mafia boss might be like if he were running a semi-pro football team in Turkey. But Berkay was a benevolent Godfather, more teddy bear than Vito Corleone. Berkay bled Stallions football. He loved the team like family. Even though growing up meant getting a real job at an international bank and scaling back his involvement on the team, he prized his role as the team's *ağabey*, or older brother.   Berkay started out playing at Marmara University before starting the Stallions team with two other friends. He bestowed the "Stallions" nickname in honor of the Italian Stallion from his beloved Rocky movies.

Berkay served as an assistant coach of sorts. I say "of sorts" because he really did not do much coaching. He rarely attended to practice, though he always had suggestions during the games. I always listened to his suggestions, but I usually stayed with my gut on tactical decisions. Our offense was effective, though usually our success could be traced to us having better players than the opposing team rather than to our coaching acumen. And though I generally stuck to my own tactical decisions, I very much appreciated Berkay's input, particularly about personnel. He knew our players well, having played with or coached them over multiple seasons. His indispensable role, however, was being able to help us manage relationships and egos on the team. Our coaching staff consisted of an offensive coordinator, a defensive coordinator, and Berkay, our *don't-let-the-Americans-tick-off-and-ruin-the-relationship-with-all-the-Turks-on-the-team* coordinator.

Managing relationships and personalities was hard work, which should be expected when multiple cultures and worldviews are blended. Jay, my fellow coach and defensive coordinator, and I both grew up or spent significant time in the American South. My roots are firmly established in South Carolina, while Jay grew up in West Virginia, Kentucky, Georgia, and Ohio. Our hometowns dotted with church steeples and American flags, we are the products of a very patriotic Southern religiosity. Our culture values the individual, hard work, merit, and efficiency. Further, we are the products of a football culture that values toughness, punctuality, sacrifice, and productivity. We threw ourselves into a landscape dotted with minarets and Turkish flags. Our players are the product of a culture that is both Muslim and nationalistic, with strong eastern roots. They prize groups and relationships and status. Further, they are the product of a soccer culture that values toughness, but that of a different variety, which is to say that running as fast as you can to hit another human being doing the same thing was not a natural move. Inevitably, our values sometimes differed.

That's where Berkay came in. He functioned as a liaison between players and coaches. Nowhere was this liaison role seen more clearly than in our hotel room in Mersin that night some players decided smoking marijuana was a good pre-game ritual. And nowhere was the difficulty of Berkay's position made more evident than this event. We had arrived on Saturday morning ahead of our Sunday afternoon game. At Berkay's strong urging our team had a strict no alcohol 48 hours prior to a game policy as well as a curfew for everyone being in their hotel rooms. Our coaching staff checked every room, which is how we noticed several players who had not arrived back at the hotel. Over a series of phone conversations we learned that four players had been out smoking marijuana. Jay and I immediately decided that they would be suspended for the game. They had broken curfew and the law, as well as impairing their ability to play and disrespected team values and those of Baba Zane who had arranged to pay for the hotel room expense. Two players, embarrassed, took their punishment in quiet acceptance, even if they disagreed. The other two players protested and insisted we let them play. We remained resolute for this behavior was unacceptable.

Berkay, though, began to act as mediator. We met over breakfast the next morning in the hotel restaurant, slowing eating the traditional morning fare of cucumbers, tomatoes, olives, bread and crumbly cheese. We sat at a table with Berkay, a couple of other team leaders and the accused players, their faces at first stoically sad and then animated in justification and defense. They desperately wanted to play. "This is my hometown, all my family are coming to see me play," remarked one player in an attempt to persuade us emotionally. "You can't suspend me for this game, I'll do extra sprints at practice," he pleaded. When those attempts failed, the group downplayed their offense. "It's not that big of a deal." Then, "you are harming the rest of the team by not letting us play." All pleas were met with a gracious, but resolute response. We informed them that our decision was final and they would not dress out for the game. I felt a twinge of guilt as we delivered the news because I genuinely liked and believed in these players and I enjoy wiping slates clean. But I knew the decision was the correct one and I appreciated Jay's steadfastness in communicating to them the universal truth that actions have consequences.

Though the previous night Berkay agreed with our decision, having talked to these players, he argued in their defense at breakfast. I could sense the difficulty of his position. He was caught in the middle. He was one of them, a Turk, not one of us Americans. Yet he was one of us, a coach, not one of the players. But he was a former player and was friends with the players. He felt pressure from both sides. The players appealed to him as a friend, valuing relationship. Jay and I appealed to him as a coach, valuing authority. I did not envy his predicament. In the end, he admitted that we all made the right decision, though I sensed that it had cost him some relational capital.

Another relational situation took us by surprise and taught us the value of status and roles within the *çevre*. Jay and I took notice that Tolga, a rookie linebacker, knew how to hit and seemed to enjoy it. We were so impressed by his play, effort, and practice attendance that we thought he deserved to start at weak-side linebacker. This announcement met immediate opposition from some of the veteran players. No one questioned Tolga's ability to play well, but several veteran players objected to a rookie getting the start. He was inexperienced and would not know how to handle game situations, or so went the argument. Other experienced players, who had not regularly attended practice and were not as talented as Tolga, should start ahead of him, they said. Their reasoning was completely at odds with my imported worldview that rewarded merit and efficiency. To me, the decision was easy. Tolga was more talented, worked harder, and attended practice more regularly than the other candidates to start. Again, Berkay was forced to act as mediator. I'm not sure how that situation would have turned out had not a foot injury kept Tolga out of the starting lineup and the game. I cannot prove it, but I do not believe that Tolga's injury was serious enough to keep him from playing. Rather, knowing the cultural rules, I think he took himself out of the situation in deference to the veteran players.

Status and roles are important to Turkish society. They were important enough to our veteran players to not allow a player without status to start. They were important enough to Tolga to take himself out of the equation and play the rookie role until he earned status (the next season he gladly started at linebacker and emerged as a leader). One of the clearest markers of status in Turkish culture is familial relationship terminology. Whereas in American culture we use the same terms—grandfather, aunt, uncle—regardless of whether they are on the maternal or paternal side of the family, Turks distinguish. And whereas in American culture we use the same term —brother or sister—to refer to siblings regardless of age, Turks distinguish. Turkish has different terms for maternal aunt and paternal aunt, for paternal uncle and for the paternal uncle who married into the family. There are different terms for older brother, older sister, younger brother, and younger sister. Grandfather on paternal side is one term, while maternal grandfather is another. Why? Because lines of authority, leadership, and honor within the family are, to some degree, decided by status and role. One friend seemed rather shocked when I told him I referred to my older brother by his name, Matt. He said he would never be able to call his older brother by his name, but only by *ağabey*, the term for older brother. To do otherwise would be disrespectful.

Coach Jay and I benefited from this status system. As Americans we had status, particularly as it related to coaching *American* football. After all, it's not called Chinese football or Kazakh football, but American football. And being American, we grew up with Chris Berman providing the soundtrack for a Deion Sanders highlight

("He. Could. Go. All. The. Way. Primetime. Primetime"). We know how to properly say "da Bears." We can throw a tight spiral and we know the difference between a waggle and a scramble and an Ickey Shuffle. In other words, simply by growing up a football fan and player in the United States, we had a knowledge and understanding of the game that warranted a measure of respect in this emerging football league. Additionally, as coaches we filled a role that was automatically awarded respect due to a cultural deference to authority. Of course, a coach must be proficient in his craft and bring a high level of acumen to his work to keep this respect and status. They could be squandered, but did not have to be initially earned.

Like any good family, no *çevre* is without dysfunction of some sort. Not everyone was willing to kiss the ring of the American coaches, showing that Turkey is no exception to the universal rule that money is the great equalizer of status. Saygun, a Koç University graduate and son of a wealthy businessman, served as the unofficial gatekeeper for American football at the university. If every good story has an antagonist, he was mine. He never quite let me all the way into his world. Respectful most of the time, he always wanted control. When he felt he had lost control, or simply was not getting his way, he would pitch what is generally referred to as a hissy fit. My last game as coach featured a sideline screaming match, in which he and another player informed Jay and me that we were the worst human beings ever in the history of human beings. Why? Because we did not let them play in the first half because they had missed more than a month of practice, a rather light punishment in my estimation. Another time, playing running back, he stopped running mid-play to complain to officials, arguing while being tackled. By their own admission Turks are typically emotional, quick to become angry. Saygun's emotions seemed to be exaggerated by family money and a superiority complex.

On the field, however, Saygun was a talented player. One of the hardest hitters on the team and unafraid of conflict or contact, he could play linebacker or free safety. Offensively, he played running back my first season with the team and performed well enough.

Against my better judgment I allowed Saygun to start the 2011-12 season at quarterback. I knew having such a volatile player, and one who did not trust me, playing quarterback would be troublesome at best, but we had no one else who could play the position that was regularly coming to practice. But after an abysmal performance in the season opener he asked to be moved to offensive guard for the next game, becoming the first player in history to play quarterback and guard in consecutive games. Only notorious heavyweights Jared Lornzen or JaMarcus Russell could have pulled that off in America.

Space does not permit to write about everybody within the Stallions's *çevre*, but to give you a glimpse into the assemblage of characters on our team allow me to briefly introduce you to several of the guys. Umbro is a pit bull of an offensive and defensive lineman, so nicknamed because he wore an Umbro brand shirt to his first practice and no one knew his real name. I still don't know it. Umbro has a great sense of humor and is mature enough to laugh at himself, which comes in handy when his friends make fun of his head, which takes a sharp 90-degree turn and is flat at the back from being strapped to a board as a baby as was custom in the east of Turkey.

Korkut Korkutoğlu has the perfect football or professional wrestling name, translated as "Scare, son of Scare." Korkut was a quiet, shy student when he first showed up to play for the Stallions. A few years later he has emerged as a leader. When Onur deployed for mandatory military service, Korkut assumed the role of team president, though his style was more managerial than smooth talking visionary. Korkut is also known for wearing inappropriate tee shirts featuring profanity or near-pornographic pictures.

Berk and Batur are two Koç University graduates who led that faction of the team. Berk filled a role as loyal deputy to Saygun and Batur. That is, he leads with them, but follows their lead, doing the grunt work. He is quite adept at getting things done and proved to be very helpful and kind. He also has a knack for nabbing interceptions — even though if you saw him lined up at cornerback you would immediately think you could beat him deep. He is not tall and doesn't appear to be fast. But he is a smart player who can read a quarterback well and break on the ball quick enough. Batur is a talented skill position player who played running back, receiver, linebacker and defensive back for us at various times. He was the go-to guy for running the reverse and was a reliable threat to break a few tackles for a long run down field. Batur was also the team's pretty boy. He drove an Audi sports car, had previously dated a celebrity fashion model, and flashed a smile whiter than the sands of Antalya. He is generally a fun guy to be around, but has an ego as big as the Bosphorus. He would tell you it's bigger.

Suat is the hard-hitting middle linebacker and even harder partier. He blitzes almost every play whether you call one or not. He is also obsessed with the television show *How I Met Your Mother*. Balıkçı, so nicknamed because the word means "fisherman" and he worked in the fishing industry, is half the man he used to be, which is not an insult to his character, but an observation of his stature. He lost over 200 pounds after gastric bypass surgery. He left our team after my first season so that he could play for a team in the first division. Hakan is still all the man he always was, which is also a comment on his stature. He is large and in charge on the defensive line, his legs like tree trunks not easily uprooted. He is also an artist, of the dark and disturbing variety. Bloody comic-book style pictures seem to be his forte. He also has a pretty cool monster voice. One of my favorite videos to show people of our football team is pre-surgery Balıkçı and Hakan swinging on a playground together while the swing set nearly comes unbolted against their combined poundage.

Lastly, I will introduce you to the two Caners. Short Caner plays free safety, runs fast, and talks even faster. Tall Caner played wide receiver and kept bringing around different girlfriends who looked almost identical to each other and making out with them on the bus to away games. He also holds the team record for tattoos, including one that looks rather homemade and features a man shooting himself in the head with blood spatter sprinkled up Caner's bicep. There are other players I could mention and others that I will write about at length elsewhere in this book, but for now the above players give you a representational sample of our team and *çevre*.

But one of the driving questions for me is *why* these players play American football. What makes them want to play an unpopular, foreign sport? What motivates them to practice in the freezing February temperatures? Why would they want to spend their free time playing such a rough sport? For many, it takes an hour or two to commute to practice. They do not receive any scholarships or money. They do not even get much fanfare as few people attend their games. So why play?

I think the answer is partially found in the concept of *çevre*. They play because they want to belong. They play for the friendship and the brotherhood. One player remarked that when you go to university you have few friends, if any, there with you. When you join the team you make friends easily, he said. Another recalled leaving one group of friends when he joined the team because he spent all his time with the football team. I recently ran into some former Stallions who are not playing this season and when asked why not, they told me that the team is not like it used to be. The friendship and brotherhood had been replaced by an incessant drive to win that saw the addition of new players from the new coach's former team that disrupted the relational order that had been established over years. There are likely many reasons why different players play, but friendship and community are the glue that holds a team together. When they depart, so do the players.

As mentioned above, Korkut was shy and quiet when he first joined the team. As they tell the story, he was awkwardly silent. One friend commented that maybe he did not really even love football, but he loved the social aspect of it. Football gave him a crew to run with and he learned social skills within that group. That friend noted the progression. At first he did not talk, but after a little while he started talking with the guys. Then he started joking, then calling people, then going out with the guys. He later became the team president and got a girlfriend. The football team gave birth to the Korkut's sociality.

For others, football was a team sport they could play. Some were swimmers or fighters prior to joining a football team. Others played basketball, but had hit a ceiling there. Many, though they love soccer, were not athletic enough to play. American football was a team sport they all could play. The competition level was not too high, older guys could still play, and a position could be earned relatively easily. Football represented a chance to be on a team, to belong, to fight for a common goal with other men to a group of guys who may have had no other outlet for such belonging. In short, these guys wanted a *çevre* and American football provided one.

Prestige is another motivation for playing American football. Players get to show off their bruises earned in tackling drills. They post their football photos to Facebook. People searching for prestige often find it outside of the mainstream. An example would be the feeling of self-superiority one feels when listening to an indie band none of his friends have heard of. Likewise, American football players take pride in rebelling against societal norms and embracing a subculture outside the mainstream. In so doing, they find the place where they belong. They find a *çevre*.

In a 2007 story for the *New York Times*, Mark St. Amant explored the motivations for Turkish students playing American football. Digging beneath the friendship answer, one player confided in him that, "I think Turks just want to belong. We're not really accepted by Europe, because they think some Muslim customs are archaic. And we're not accepted by the Middle East because they feel that we aren't Muslim enough. We don't really belong anywhere."

It is to that national search for a *çevre* on the global stage that we now turn.

5

EUROPEAN DREAMS

The Turkish language has a handy tense whereby one can make a statement without having to accept responsibility for the accuracy or truthfulness of said statement. Grammar books refer to it as the *reported tense*, but I like to call it the "I heard this from somebody else so don't blame me if it is incorrect" tense. Such reportage is designated by appending the suffix -miş/-muş to the end of the verb. Its kind of like when old Southern ladies say, *"Well you didn't hear it from me, but I heard...."* before sharing the latest gossip. I bring it up because I am not sure how much of the following story is true. But I'm going to tell you anyway and you cannot hold me responsible if it is not completely accurate because I'm telling you beforehand that it is a miş/muş story. Got it? Good. Do you see why I love this tense? So, without any further ado, *you didn't hear it from me, but...*

A few months after taking over as the Stallions coach we held our first scrimmage. The night before I spoke via phone to the opponent's coach, also an American. We hammered out the details of how we wanted to handle the scrimmage and chatted a bit about our experiences living in Turkey. He was particularly disappointed in his experience with Turkish ladies because, reportedly, he was forced to punt, if you get what I'm saying. I thought the comment odd, but filed it away in my mind under "things loser men from Arizona say." The following day I watched as this coach absolutely berated his players and treated them like dogs. Now, I have not lived a sheltered life, but I had never before heard such cutting language. I'm pretty sure he invented a few new cuss words. I realize some coaches are more Sergeant Hartman than Sergeant Pepper, but this guy was over the top. Worse for him, all his hysterics and cussing and berating helped him none. We beat him 35-0.

This is where the story gets *-miş/-muş*. Later that season this coach left his team, the Istanbul Cavaliers, in the middle of the season, in the middle of a practice. You didn't hear this from me, but I heard he took a water break and never returned. He did not just leave the team, he left the country, going to that notorious football haven, Finland. Some players cited problems with the team president as the reason for his exit, while others cited the Istanbul female population's shutdown defense. Whatever the details of his departure were, I know for certain that he left in the middle of the season because I was asked to coach the Cavs in their European league games that spring, an overture I politely declined.

Fast-forward a year to the summer of 2012. I resigned as the Stallions coach to focus on other projects, this book being one of them. Who do the players track down to come coach the team? Yep, ol' Coach Potty Mouth. I wondered why would they want him when he treated his players like street dogs. Why would they hire him when he deserted his previous team in the middle of the season, leaving the team to disintegrate? Why would they favor this guy when they had the opportunity to have a former North Carolina State University starting quarterback come to coach and play for the team? Why? Because he had connections to Europe.

And they have European dreams.

Turkey's location between East and West has fostered an identity crisis over the last century. Cultural streams from all directions have flowed into Turkey for generations. Turks find themselves too modern for much of Central Asia and the Middle East. Europeans find Turks too Muslim, while the Muslim world does not think they are Muslim enough. They have one foot in two very different worlds, totally belonging to neither.

Some observers of Turkey suggest the East meets West paradigm is a cliché way of looking at Turkey, a bit overdone. But clichés exist because they contain enough truth to keep them alive as viable explanations of reality. And the East meets West paradigm is very much a part of modern Turkey, and in particular, this phenomenon is nowhere more noticeable than in Istanbul. One day my wife and I were driving on a major city highway between the skyscrapers of neighboring financial districts when we noticed a cow grazing in the median between the highway and frontage road. Off another major thoroughfare we've spotted shepherds herding sheep. Yet it is not uncommon to also see a stable full of BMWs and Audis, or even the occasional Lamborghini, racing these same highways. Complementing luxury cars, designer fashion is found all over the city on billboards, magazine covers, and ladies on the subway. Istanbul has more shopping malls than Bill Belichick has hoodies, including a seven-story behemoth that was once the largest mall in all of Europe. Yet each neighborhood also has a weekly outdoor market where the masses buy imitation designer clothes alongside their weekly produce. Here, "Adidas" track pants run about four dollars.

My favorite example of East meeting West is the hospital where our son was born. It is a high-technology, modern hospital where many of the doctors have been trained in the United States or London. We received care in this hospital that was just as good as we would have received back home, maybe better. Further, the place had big-city swank appeal. I often mistakenly referred to our patient room as a hotel room. When it came time for our last meal before being discharged, hospital staff brought linen-covered table and chairs, a flower arrangement and a silver cloche-covered three-course meal to celebrate the birth of our son. I've never seen that in

America! Yet, for all its swank, technology, and western training, eastern animism and superstition is still very present. The *nazar* bead, a eye-shaped charm to protect against the Evil Eye spiritual force, is subtly woven into the decor of the hospital on ceilings and floors to protect the hospital against evil spirits. Without knowledge of the *nazar* charm one would not even notice its presence. But there it is, all over the hospital, as if to say "just in case."

Istanbulites see themselves as Europeans and, technically, half the city resides on the European continent. The beautiful Bosphorus Strait divides both city and continents. In many initial conversations with Turks in which they are describing their country to me, they go to great lengths to point out that Turkey is "like Europe." Its citizens are open-minded, educated, and modern, they explain. They go to even greater lengths to distance themselves from Arabs who are, as the party line goes, not as modern or clean as the Turks. In some ways, their pining to put on European airs is an effort to establish rapport with the westerner and put a reputable face on the country as if every westerner believed that *modern* always equals *better*. But that desire to put up a good face to the westerner by being "modern" betrays some deep-seated embarrassment over their Central Asian heritage. Fueled by this shame, some Istanbulites mock their past and their countryside as primitive and embrace the vision of a sophisticated European future.

The longing for Europe in the hearts of many Turks is the fruit of the Atatürkian dream. Atatürk had a flair for things western, both in his vices and his politics. His underwear was imported from France, his drinks alcoholic, and his women many. He held much of Turkey's Ottoman past in disdain. He scrapped the Islamic caliphate, the Arabic script, the fez hat, and the veils covering women's faces. Atatürk was obsessed with Turkey entering the world's mainstream and tirelessly worked to westernize his young republic. The country set out to enact policies befitting a "civilized" nation.

Atatürk's heirs continue to vigorously pursue his quest for Western acceptance. Turkey has tried for decades to gain acceptance into the European Union, though it has yet to attain membership.

There are likely many reasons why their bid has stalled, including human rights issues involving ethnic and religious minorities, economic factors, geopolitical tensions with Greece, and general European fear of allowing more than 70 million Muslims unfettered border access. But while the politics of European Union membership play out in bureaucratic time, a large segment of the Turkish public continues to pursue a cultural alignment with Europe, adopting its architecture, dress, entertainment, education, and secularism.

A national maxim has emerged that to be European is to be modern. To be modern is to be superior, enlightened even. Association with Europe, then, brings prestige. So when the opportunity presented itself to some of our Stallions players to join the Cavs for their European league games in 2011, all who were invited jumped at the chance. They explained to me that it was an "honor" to play in a European league game. It was "prestigious." Playing in the game was a source of national and personal pride.

It meant they belonged.

It meant they, as individuals, belonged in Europe and that Turkey, as a nation, belonged in Europe, if even just for four quarters.

Being from America, where our interest in Europe is relegated to backpacking vacations and making French jokes, coaching in the European league had less appeal to me. I declined an invitation to coach the coach-less Cavs, preferring to focus my energies on our own team. But I did attend the game to support those Stallions playing in their European premiere. The opposing team was from Serbia, a place I know somewhere between zero and zilch about. What I know of Serbia comes from movies, where Serbs are often typecast as terrorists or militants, and from a concert I happened upon several years ago in Romania. About the time we walked onto the grounds of a Woodstock-like festival, a band member waved Serbia's flag and screamed, "Eff you, America!," except he used four letters to say eff. Let's just say that the Serbs are not known for their hospitality. So when I saw the size and toughness of the Serbian squad it fit my stereotype.

The Cavs made the game into an event. A deejay kept the music going from a party truck parked beside the field. Cheerleaders cheered on the sidelines and danced midfield at halftime in ways that would get them honor-killed in other Muslim countries. Red Bull sponsored the game, a hint that football is more akin to an extreme sport than a mainstream offering in Turkey. Unfortunately, the Cavs got manhandled in the game. Most of the Stallions did not get to play very much, settling for catch-up duty in the second half. At one point I noticed Korkut eating a hamburger on the sidelines, a sign that he was not anticipating his number being called anytime soon. Saygun entered the game at running back with the ball on his own five-yard line. A defensive player rushed through the line of scrimmage, took the ball straight out of his hands, and walked into the end zone, easy peasy. The Cavs had no coach, a fact that only intensified the sideline chaos. The Serbs had some Americans playing for their team and the one playing running back may as well have been Adrian Peterson with the way he dominated up the middle and around the end. The one bright spot on an otherwise dark game was the defensive effort put out by the Stallions players when they finally took the field together. They acquitted themselves quite well, which made Jay and me the right kind of proud.

The fallout from that game was more than any of the players could have anticipated that day. The Cavs team basically disintegrated, at least for a while. They did not have enough players to travel to Europe for any of their remaining league games and had to forfeit those games, a move that resulted in all Turkish teams being banned from the league for one year. Thus, the Stallions' 2012 bid to play in the league in was stuffed like a run up the middle on fourth down.

Turks have found a glimmer of recent success in Europe, however. In 2012, the national team traveled to Romania and defeated the Romanian national team. Then in 2013 the Stallions, equipped with a few American imports of their own, traveled to Serbia for a friendly match and brought a 30-20 victory back home, exacting some measure of revenge. It is unclear whether Korkut ate any hamburgers on the sideline of this match.

If recent trends hold true, Turkish teams will continue to press into Europe, recalling their Seljuk ancestors of old. But instead of being a dreaded foe intent on conquering, these Turks are looking to assimilate themselves and their culture into that of Europe. To do so would give them a sense of prestige and a proper place to belong.

Two questions arise as one envisions a future where Turkey is fully counted among Europe, expressed politically with admittance to the European Union, economically in its trade agreements, and culturally in reciprocal acceptance on the part of Europeans. The first question is whether Europeanization is even possible for Turkey. The second question is whether such a move would even be good.

It is unlikely that Turkey will make the leap from Central Asian to wide acceptance as European in the foreseeable future. Even if Turkey is granted membership in the European Union, a prospect that neither side seems to be currently pursuing with great diligence, wide acceptance of European Turkey is not guaranteed. Rather, such a move would likely be seen as the stuff of political and economic convenience for both parties. Governments—and the financial interests that sustain them—make such agreements, but citizens and neighbors determine culture on the ground. Political rule does not get at the root of culture-making assumptions and ideas. Geopolitics may bind peoples together at a certain level for a period of time, but, as we observed at the breakup of the Soviet Union, they do not unite. The former Soviet states of Central Asia were neither Russianized nor accepted as truly Russian.

The reason that Turkey will likely never be truly European is that cultures and nations follow trajectories and the trajectories of Europe and Turkey are different because they have different starting points. Europe, once barbaric, was converted to Christianity more than a thousand years ago. As such, even with its modern secularism, its history and worldview follow a trajectory from Christianity. Turkey, on the other hand, has its roots deeply embedded in animism and Islam and its trajectory springs forth from these. Even though modern-day pluralists insist that religion is religion no matter the stripe, Christianity and Islam are fundamentally different and produce fundamentally different societies that are often at odds with one another. Samuel Huntington is famous for making this point in "The Clash of Civilizations and the Remaking of World Order," in which he argued that civilizations are not coming closer together but are being driven farther apart on the basis of cultural and religious identity.

Further, even though Turkey is very much secularized in many respects, the speed of its disposal of formal religion has not kept pace with Europe. In fact, the trend in Turkey over the last fifteen years has been to embrace Islam even more. The current government, Prime Minister Recep Erdoğan's Justice and Development Party, is known as an Islamic party, albeit more moderate than others. Fifteen years ago, I am told that you would hardly see any women with their heads covered on the street. Today, roughly fifty percent cover their heads. Publicly funded mosques are being erected around the country, even if they are sparsely attended. The call to prayer rings out in deafening tones from all directions five times per day. Animistic superstition to charm away evil is on wide display along every street: the nazar bead on walls, busses, and babies; sitting on thin strips of newspaper to protect against infertility; Quranic passages and prayer blessings written in Arabic and displayed in shops for protection; and statues of elephants or turtles to bring good luck to businesses.

Additionally, the path the government will choose relating to Europe is unclear. Will it pursue membership in the European Union or ally itself with states decidedly outside of Europe both geographically and philosophically, like Iran? With such questions floating in the air like a balloon over Cappadocia it is hard to imagine Turkey being accepted as one of the boys in Europe any time soon.

Let us consider for a moment, however, that Turkey could, if it so chose, be assimilated into Europe. Would this be a good thing? In some respects, yes, this would be good. The harmonization of cultures and peoples is a good thing. If ethnic and religious minorities are given greater human rights, this would also be a mark in the positive column. Potential economic benefits of partnership are also a plus. But I dare not argue for an abandonment of all that is at home in Turkish and Central Asian culture. Not everything modern is better.

If, in an attempt to keep pace with Europe, Turks lost their deeply relational and communal culture I would be very disappointed. Turks are known to show over-the-top hospitality to friend and guest alike. I once met a man named Ali in a neighborhood shop that sold electrical supplies. He pointed in the direction of his nearby apartment and told me to stop by sometime. Weeks later I was walking with my wife and son near his apartment and we decided to drop in. We knocked on his door hoping we had not mistaken his apartment for someone else's. Ali's wife opened the door with trepidation, unsure of her obviously foreign visitors. Like many Turkish men Ali works on the crew of a large ship and spends much of each year sailing in nearby seas. His wife initially assumed I was a Russian colleague of her husband and I surmised she was worried I had come to cause trouble. Her countenance lightened when she noticed I was accompanied by my wife and toddler son. She and her daughter came outside and she invited us to sit and drink tea on her tiled patio while we waited for Ali to return home. When he arrived we all went inside and they insisted we stay for dinner, which consisted of olive oil braised green beans and a side of rice pilaf. Though we did not know this family well at all, they were quick to invite us into their home and share a meal with us. Such hospitality is not atypical. The non-urban roots of the Turkish public cultivated a culture that values family relationships, long hours spent together and an unhurried pace of life. It would be a shame to lose these in any assimilation project.

Though my own religious views see a different ordering of the spiritual world than many of my Turkish friends would subscribe to, I appreciate their awareness of the unseen spiritual forces at work in our world. We have mostly lost this awareness in the West and it is unfortunate when a worldview that does not allow for that which is unseen mocks the long-held spiritual awareness of religious cultures.

Such qualities and values are different, if not at odds, with those of much of popular Europe. A belief in God or an awareness of the spiritual world is not primitive in the derogatory sense. Rather, it is foundational wisdom of old, to be respected. Large village families are not backward but recognize that we were not created to be alone but to be a part of a larger community, the most foundational of which is the family. The slow pace of Anatolian life reflects a belief that there are other important things in life besides work and money. If assimilation into Europe meant bending away from these aspects of Turkish culture, it would not be a good thing. These qualities and values may seem antiquated to some, lacking in prestige. But not everything old is bad and not everything new is good. I would prefer that Turkey, while always critically learning from its global neighbors, cultivate what already makes it unique and beautiful.

But what about Turkish American football? Much in the same way that Turkey as a nation is not likely to assimilate into Europe in the foreseeable future, it is unlikely that Turkish American football teams are poised to succeed at a high level in Europe. A broad and deep talent pool of capable players has just not been developed yet, though this hardly means that it cannot be done. Can Turkish teams succeed in the European leagues? Should they even try?

I recommend a few steps to help American football to succeed in Europe and build its brand in Turkey:

1. A collaborative effort to build and send a Turkish national or all-star team to regularly compete in Europe should continue. Individual club teams do not have currently enough talented players at all positions to consistently compete in meaningful ways against Europe's tougher competition. Pooling the available talent into national or all-star teams is a viable way to field competitive teams.

2. The governing federation should use available funds to market the team in a patriotic manner. That is, tap into the abundant national pride of the Turkish public to support the

team. Turks may not know or care much for American football, but they love and care deeply for Turkey and its reputation abroad.

3. The federation should use this exposure to secure sponsorships from Turkish corporations and then use these funds to upgrade facilities, purchase new equipment, and invest in player development in order to improve the quality of play in the Turkish league.

4. A concerted effort to multiply the new interest in Turkish American football by utilizing social media should be applied. Turks use social media at high rates, so a creative social media push could create viral interest in the sport.

5. Club teams should refocus to prioritize the quality of play in the Turkish league over participation in the European league for a time. Doing so the sport will have a better opportunity to grow and recruit more and better athletes to play, which will increase the quality of play. As the quality increases, popularity—and the accompanying sponsorship monies—are more likely to follow. Securing a foundation is a basic principle to building most anything, and Turkey's American football foundation is not sure yet. Foundations cannot be skipped in construction and should not be skipped in building a competitive football league.

But this book is not necessarily about what could or should be. This book is about what is. And so, regardless of my plan for success, club teams will continue to venture into Europe because the current group of players has European dreams. For a segment of Turkey's population, mostly that which is urban and socially mobile, association with Europe brings prestige, a sense of belonging, and a reason to boast. Whether such prestige and belonging turns out to be fleeting, lasting or even real is not the point. The point is that it is perceived and pursued.

In this way American football is simply a mirror of the pining toward Europe from some corners of the culture. American football in Turkey and its pursuit of belonging illustrates a larger national identity crisis in Turkey. To which direction will Turkey turn politically, economically, and culturally? Will it look East or West? Or will it forge its own identity as a third culture country—a blend of East and West—and be comfortable enough to wear that skin on the world stage and at home?

The answers are unclear, but chances are Turkey will not be eating hamburgers on the sideline.

ÇAY BREAK

First Game

Beneath the thick December gray
and the cold winter's wind
it was a to-remember day
for the Stallions entered in
to the field of play.

they hit, they blocked and tackled.
they ran and hit like war.
they bent but never crackled,
stayed steady to their core.

they're a brotherhood of blood,
a fraternity of fight.
no one from another 'hood
would escape the night.

so when the gray had settled
and the whistles blew no more,
the Stallions were victorious,
22-6 the final score

—written December 2010 after my first game coaching the Stallions

6

CARPET FIELDS AND
VOLLEYBALL KNEE PADS

Growing up in the American South there were a number of things I grew accustomed to experiencing that might seem peculiar to an outsider. Some were innocently glorious, like generous sweet tea and free refills of it, neither of which is a guarantee elsewhere. Others were rubberneckingly curious, like the eclectic assortment of characters at a camp-style seafood house, a lot that defies description by words alone. Where I grew up, a rebel-flagged pickup truck blaring alternating country and rap music was not an antinomy, but simply normal. Southerners' near religious devotion to football, however, is no longer among our peculiarities. There was a time when the South was football's Holy Land. Neyland Stadium and The Cotton Bowl were among its cathedrals, the players its priests, and Bear Bryant its major prophet. But now, the entire country has been evangelized and football has usurped baseball as America's favorite sport, the rise of the NFL as premier television event its greatest apologetic. Ulysses Everett McGill might even describe football itself as a geographical oddity, first and ten from everywhere.

At the risk of sacrilege, there seems to be something almost spiritual about a football Friday night or a Saturday in the South, as if God intended the sport as a gift of common grace; an arena where boys grow into men and men relive boyhood, where communities and campuses rally together with a very real, if only temporary, unity. For those three hours neither race nor class matters, only the team. And though we may have marred this gift, as humans are wont to do, with money, greed, power, and sex (see *NFL, The*), there remains a remnant of integrity and honor in the sport. August two-a-days don't lie.

Football exudes pageantry. Large collegiate bands provide the soundtrack to a hundred outdoor cocktail parties, ESPN's Kirk Herbstreit the master of ceremonies. Extravagant tailgates line parking lots and fairgrounds, complete with RVs, TVs, and enough fried chicken to feed Texas A&M's entire Twelfth Man. Upwards of 100,000 people might attend a single game. Less amplified, but no less important, are the high school games that are a staple of Friday night life in small towns across America. As the sweltering heat of summer gives way to fall, the October chill and a playoff run are most welcomed guests. Dew settles in on freshly cut grass. Fog hangs thick, like bad news, across the field. The sounds of whistles and cheerleaders and French horns fill the air. Fathers holler at referees, while coaches holler at the boys who holler at each other. Whether all of it is cacophony or chorus, it brings back fond memories and makes this Turkey-residing heart homesick.

All this to say, football in America is an event, a spectacle. And we have not even mentioned the Super Bowl and all its excess. But in Turkey, if American football is a spectacle at all, it is because it is so out of place, so not at home, so not an event. Mostly the sport is ignored or unknown, mistaken for baseball or rugby. Usually, the only frame of reference for the sport is football films and the lasting impression is the roughness of the game. Turkish sports fans, under the intoxicating influence of a soccer culture, find such athletic violence strange, which makes sense if you have ever witnessed

Christiano Ronaldo alternate between superhuman footballer and middle school drama queen with a broken heart, which is to say that he whines with such hysteria that even the Republicans feel sorry for him. Any population whose favorite sport features players rolling on the turf in extreme agony as if peppered by machine gun fire when only slightly tripped will probably not readily embrace a sport that features the likes of Ray Lewis. American football stands out for its voluntary violence.

Many young Turks, however, have grown to love the hitting. They are the ones who keep this niche sport alive and growing. Suat, our middle linebacker, is tougher than beef jerky. He loves to hit, plays hurt, and will blitz every play whether we call it or not. Fatih, one of our smallest players, never met a bigger player who made him flinch. He might not make the tackle, but he would definitely make the hit. In fact, the DNA of Turkish football is tough and rugged, seeing as during the first decade of the sport in Turkey they played without pads. Unfortunately, that DNA has not been transferred to all newcomers. Tackling at times more closely resembled hugging than hitting. Some players had difficulty with the idea of one man running full steam into another man, who also happened to be running full steam. Collision, it turns out, is a learned behavior.

Soccer's influence is not only limited to an aversion to hitting. The structure of the league is taken from the majority sport. Teams are split into two divisions. Like soccer, teams fluctuate between divisions based on performance. At season's end the bottom two first division teams play a "play-out" match against the top two teams from the second division, with the winners competing in the first division the following season. As odd as this system may seem to the American fan's palate, I find it intriguing. Late season snooze-fest games between NFL bottom feeders (here's looking at you, Cleveland and Buffalo) would be much more fun if relegation to a lesser league was at stake.

A blessing of coaching in a nation of soccer fanatics was the relative ease of finding capable placekickers and punters. Never in my coaching career have I ever seen such fierce competition to be the kicker, nor such prestige assigned to the position. "No, I'm the punter!" What is a fringe position in the United States is a coveted one in Turkey. Unfortunately, finding goalposts proved to be more difficult than finding kickers. Not all fields were equipped with them and the ones that were usually only had one set, located behind one of the end zones, forcing teams to switch directions in order to attempt a field goal or an extra point. Ironically, I never called for a field goal in two years of coaching the best kickers I have ever coached, and we always went for two.

Soccer culture's best contribution to American football in Turkey, however, is its fan culture. We did not always draw many fans to our games, but when we did they came singing and chanting. Soccer fans are the same the world over. Hooliganism knows no borders, but many languages. I attended a soccer match once. I went through more security at that stadium than in many airports. They do not even let fans bring lose change into the stadium, lest one pelt a player with it. And if one person were to hurl a lira coin at a player, the masses would likely follow. It is not that Turkish culture is overly violent, but rather, communal. What one person does, many do. And so a stadium, fueled by passion and perhaps ignited by that lethal combination of poor officiating and alcohol, can turn violent quickly. But if they have no coins to throw, what will they do? Rip bolted stadium seats up and throw them onto the field? Of course they will! Light flares and toss them? Why not?! Run onto the field and try to fight even though there are police shoulder to shoulder guarding the field? Do I really have to answer? No matter the rules, a fan will always find a way to protest, and a soccer fan will do so with flair. Or flares.

Granted, this behavior is the exception to the rule. Generally, soccer fans pour their passion into singing, chanting, and cursing a blue streak. Cursing, as it turned out, was exactly what got fans of our university team banned for a game. Yes, sport federations in Turkey sometimes ban fans from attending games. Galatasaray, one of the largest and most popular soccer clubs in Turkey, recently opened a prized 50,000-seat stadium but played one of its first games in the new arena in front of zero fans due to a punitive ban. I watched part of the game on television and the silence was eerie. I do not know what our university team's fans said to deserve the ban—I am not well versed in Turkish profanity—but the game officials had the authority to turn them in to the federation, which handed down the ban. Of course, banning a Turkish American football team's fans is less drastic than it might seem since only fifty or so people were normally in attendance. In this case, the silence was all too familiar.

Sometimes, however, players were able to turn out enough friends to attend that the atmosphere became rather festive, like the Cavaliers' Red Bull-sponsored Serbian match and dance party mentioned in chapter five. Championship games always draw raucous crowds. Unfortunately, our normal games generally had forty or fifty friends and passersby watching the game while nibbling sunflower seeds and chatting. Not exactly LSU's Death Valley.

Soccer bequeathed one more thing to American football in Turkey—the fields. There are no designated American football fields in Turkey so games are played on soccer pitches and the field dimensions vary. Our home field was a "carpet field," an artificially surfaced field caged in by a 30-foot-tall chain link fence. Carpet fields are scattered throughout the city for recreation league soccer matches. Where there are no carpet fields, kids just play in the street using a couple of rocks to mark each goal. Our carpet field was almost 100 yards long. The distance between yard lines—painted yellow to not be mistaken for the white soccer lines—measured just under five yards. Some fields were more exact than others. The one in Mersin was exactly 90 yards so midfield was the 45-yard line. The end zones were seven yards deep. Painted or chalked lines were a luxury as some teams found it more convenient to mark the lines with athletic tape, which came unglued faster than an ACC defense. As we arrived in the parking lot in Ankara, the nation's capital, to play in the 2011 play-out match I was excited to see the large soccer stadium and I looked forward to playing on a well-kept grass field with painted lines. Then our bus driver kept driving. Much to my dismay, we did not play on the well-manicured soccer pitch but on an adjacent practice field where the lines were straps of canvas staked into the ground. Amazingly, no one tripped or tore a ligament.

American football clubs often do not have enough money to fund such an expensive sport. The sponsorship lira they do collect usually goes toward equipment and travel. As such, there is not always enough money to paint the field. Or the field managers do not want American football lines cluttering their soccer fields. The athletic tape or canvas yard lines reveal an admirable trait about Turks. They find ways to get things done, even in the face of obstacles. My family calls this "O.D.'ing" something, after my granddaddy, O.D. Park, who once rigged his car engine with chewing gum to get to the airport on time. Others call it life hacking and Turks are experts at the practice. Our university, not having the proper equipment to line the field, used a paint roller to life hack the yard lines fifteen minutes prior to kickoff. Turks can "health hack" it, too. Once, when a player broke his finger, they used a small teaspoon as a splint. Another time a player broke his leg during practice and was taken to a government hospital. According to hospital staff some equipment was stolen from a supply closet, so, while he was awaiting surgery, the two sections of his fibula were held in place by a small rope weighted by a five-liter water jug.

Their life hacking skills are most useful in getting the most out of available equipment. In our team's early days they only owned fifteen helmets. The offense and defense would alternate use of the helmets, and when a player would sub in he would often take the helmet of the exiting player. This practice added a whole new degree of difficulty for the coach who not only had to substitute for skill but also had to factor in head sizes.

Though American football equipment comes scarce in Turkey, the federation requires players to wear proper equipment to play. In fact, referees inspect each player prior to each game to ensure everyone is wearing all the required pads. I found the whole process interesting. In between team warm ups and the coin toss, game officials would call the team together for a license and equipment check. Every player is required to have a federation-issued license, which can be obtained with thirty lira and a physical examination by a doctor, the exam often life hacked by a doctor simply signing the form without performing an actual exam. During the check, the entire team stands in a line facing the officials. One official will call each player by name, check his license, and send him to the equipment check. There, each player is frisked to make sure he has all his pads, tail pad included. Players enliven the process with cheers, chants, struts, and high-fives as if this were the starting lineups being announced. The problem with the equipment check is that our players often did not have enough leg pads for everyone on the roster. This is where Turkish ingenuity and life hacking comes in to play. Players would stuff scraps of other pads or some sort of foam into their pants for the inspection. Knee pads became thigh pads and helmet liner padding was ripped into makeshift tailbone pads. Anything that remotely resembled padding could be used, so long as some form of matter was there to be felt when the referee frisked them. After the equipment check our sideline would be littered with scraps of pads and foam as players chucked them out. The whole thing was a ruse and a waste of time.

For pure comedic value, my favorite equipment life hack was Saygun's insistence on wearing volleyball knee pads over his football pants, even though we had real knee pads available. Picture with me, for just a minute, Peyton Manning outfitted with volleyball knee pads and, perhaps, a hoodie underneath his shoulder pads to keep warm. You now have an idea of how our team sometimes looked. Jerseys are usually uniform, but helmet and pant colors are often mismatched. At various times, though our colors were red and black, we had players outfitted in green, purple, orange, and silver pants or helmets. When the federation recently mandated uniform helmet colors we spray-painted some of our off-helmets black, while others were colored by automobile painters. What else are you going to do when American football equipment is so expensive and hard to come by? You play with what you have. You hack it.

American football equipment is not manufactured in Turkey, therefore all equipment must be imported. As such, it is very expensive, roughly twice the cost of the same equipment in the United States. During our first year we lacked enough quality helmets to outfit our team properly so we ordered fifty Riddell Revolution helmets from America and had them shipped to us. This decision turned out to be the source of much weeping and gnashing of teeth. It was also quite the lesson in Turkish culture, business, and government. Frustration from these helmets would follow me like one of Istanbul's stray dogs.

The helmets were shipped in boxes of sixteen, leaving two helmets not in the main shipment. Those two helmets were delivered by the post office to an assistant coach's apartment with instructions on where to pick up the remaining forty-eight. I went with that coach to pick up the helmets, but they would not give them to us because the shipment was in another coach's name. When that coach went to pick them up they would not give them to him either because the number of helmets and weight of the shipment listed on the official papers did not match what was physically in the depot. Of course, the reason they did not match was because they had already delivered two of the helmets. We offered to bring those two helmets back to add to the shipment, but that offer was denied. Later, they told us the helmets had been moved to another depot in another part of the city and were available for pickup. The helmets were not there when we arrived and as best we can tell they had never been there. Anybody know the Turkish translation for "wild goose chase"?

Like most problems this one could be traced to money. Officially, the government was going to charge a huge customs fee if we imported the helmets. Turkey's protectionist economic policies necessitate unfair taxes on imports. Electronics are hit the worst, often causing prices to be two or three times higher than in the United States. The idea is to set the price point for foreign items so high that its citizenry will be persuaded to buy Turkish-made products. However, no Turkish-made American football helmets exist. Still, habit dictates policy and so there was a huge tax. Further, taxes are high on imports because it is one of the ways the government can be sure to collect taxes. Most store and restaurant owners only pay sales taxes if the customer pays with a credit card, thus leaving an electronic trail. Otherwise, taxes are largely ignored. One might say they "life hack" the tax system. So high import taxes ensure revenue for the government, which is both a curse and a blessing. They are a curse because the taxes are such that they seem burdensome or unnecessarily punitive. They are a blessing because, unlike many countries in the region, Turkey enjoys reliable public transportation, a decent economy, and a stable government. Regardless, I did not want our players to be taxed out of proper protective equipment and that seemed to be the case.

Though I cannot prove it, I believe customs agents gave us the runaround because they were fishing for a bribe, a common practice at all levels of government the world over. Just weeks before we attempted to import these helmets a government sting brought down a sophisticated bribery operation among customs agents. In other cases I have heard of police officers collecting "soup money" from would-be traffic offenders to pay for their lunch. However, we were absolutely unwilling to pay a bribe, thus agents shuffled us from one warehouse to another giving us various reasons why we could not take the helmets. Like a good rushing attack designed to wear down the defense, they were trying to frustrate us into submission, which they eventually did. We ended up having to pay to ship the helmets back to America and have visiting friends pack them in a few extra bags. To add insult to injury, we also had to pay the customs department storage fees for the months that the helmets sat in their warehouse while we angled to get them out. The lesson, as always, governments will get your money no matter what.

If bribery is woven into Turkish culture, there is also a built-in workaround called *torpil*. Torpil is best translated as having an inside track or having the ability to pull strings to get what you want accomplished. It is the old adage *"it's not what you know, but who you know"* on Lance Armstrong-level steroids. For example, torpil is the only possible explanation for how former USC coach Lane Kiffin, son of longtime and well-respected coach Monte Kiffin, keeps getting head coaching jobs despite his consistent losing or how Tori

Spelling ever had a television career. Sometimes torpil works better than other times. Saygun, whose father is a wealthy and connected businessman, thought he might have torpil with the customs agents guarding the helmets so we drove to the warehouse to press the agents. Unfortunately, we did not have torpil with the right people in this situation and it was all to no avail. However, in my second season we had several players who applied for their license late and had not received it by the first game. The referees were not going to allow those players to participate in the game. One player, Ege, knew a federation official and had a good relationship with him. He telephoned the official and made his case for why the players should be allowed to play. The official informed the referees that they players were eligible. Torpil won that day.

Sometimes torpil crept on to the field in ways I was uncomfortable with. Some veteran players felt they should have starting positions guaranteed simply because they had been on the team longer, with no respect to actual talent or even practice attendance. In the team's early days, one player quit the team because there was no torpil. This cultural phenomenon does not mesh well with football, a sport that rewards talent, effort, and toughness above relational connectedness and status.

American football in Turkey, thus, retains much of the sport's essence regardless of the culture in which it is played. However, with torpil, equipment issues, hacks, fanfare, and soccer's influence the sport definitely takes on a distinct Turkish flavor, making for a unique experience all around. In the next chapter, we will explore the contours of this experience in more detail.

7

TWENTY-FIVE YARDS FROM THE BALL

Take a trip with me.

We're going to a Stallions game, perhaps in Izmir or Ankara. We'll board a bus and drive all Friday night, stopping at various times for tea and soup and cigarettes. We'll arrive too early to check in to our hotel so we'll walk by the sea, eating sunflower seeds—one at a time, of course—and tossing the football around. We'll nap in the afternoon and enjoy a huge team meal in the evening, local fare, famous throughout the world if you listen to the waiter. Sunday morning we'll get up early by Turkish standards, around 9 a.m., and eat cucumbers, tomatoes, bread, honey, and cheese for breakfast before boarding a bus to the stadium. We'll get lost on the way and arrive late. Since you are accompanying me you will witness me completely stressed out over a number of issues: "do we have enough equipment?," "who actually showed up today?," "I've still got to make a depth chart," "the team is taking forever to get dressed and we only have 25 minutes before kickoff" and "my quarterback is wearing volleyball knee pads!" Eventually, in the greatest upset since Bill Belichick won the conversationalist of the year award, all our players will get dressed and we will have enough equipment to outfit everybody.

We'll make our way from the locker room to the field to see what surprises await. Because American football is an emerging sport, there are no fields or stadiums designated specifically for football in Turkey. Fields are marked by great variance between them. We have played games on normal grass and a plethora of artificial surfaces. Some fields are caged in by high chain link fencing. Some are large soccer stadiums. One, you remember from earlier, was a pasture. Adjacent to one field was a mosque under construction that kids used for an upper deck, kind of like the apartment-top seating next to Wrigley Field, but with much less alcohol. Some fields are 100 yards long, some slightly less. Some yard lines are painted, some are taped. No standard exists.

The style of the game harkens back to a different era of football in the United States. Most teams run simple, conservative sets that feature the running game as the Turkish passing game lags terribly, like a little brother who never can quite catch up to his older siblings. This, of course, is to be expected in a soccer nation. Passing and catching utilize the hands, often under threat of a shot to the ribs. Corner kicks do not. Additionally, aspects of the game that feel innate to an American who has watched football from the womb go over like suggesting the Greeks invented baklava in Turkey. For instance, I tried implementing a new cadence that included the ability to audible to new plays if the defense gave us a nasty look. You would have thought I'd asked them to solve Conway's tangle or best Pythagoras for a better theorem. We were resigned to *"down, set, hut."* It is not an issue of smarts—the Turks are plenty smart, especially these private school footballers—but an issue of familiarity. While I had the luxury of learning to change the play at the line in seventh grade, they did not. Later, we did install a simplified audible system so that we could change any play to one of a set number of plays assigned to a color or city.

Great disparity exists between experienced teams and newly formed teams. As the sport grows in popularity and access to NFL games increases, the Turkish playbook is expanding well beyond the standard I-formation and the toss sweep for teams that feature a core group of veteran players. Bored with simplicity and exposed to more complex offenses via Internet video, these teams are willing to try new approaches and have a higher capacity for absorbing new schemes. They are implementing aspects of spread, speed option, and wildcat offenses, while passing more and introducing multiple formations. Other teams, however, struggle to simply line up correctly. We played one first-year team that lined up to receive each kickoff 25 yards from the ball. We noticed it on the opening kickoff and I gave the kicker a nod to kick the ball onside, which we easily recovered. After scoring quickly against a porous defense we again lined up to kick. Again, they were 25 yards from the ball, a formation they repeated each kickoff. Seeing that they were a first-year team and that we were going to win handily, Coach Jay and I exercised restraint and only allowed an onside kick every other kickoff. Eventually, we tried to coach up their players a bit and instructed them to move up to the standard distance of ten yards from the ball. Those players near our sideline did so, but were immediately "corrected" from their sideline and told to move back. I felt little mercy after that and we eventually won 70-7. In theory we could have kept possession of the ball the entire game. We could have just kept scoring, kicking and recovering onside kicks, and repeating the process. But then our defense would have been bored and I would have felt like slimy Florida Steve Spurrier for running the score up so much (as opposed to the respectable Steve Spurrier who now coaches my beloved South Carolina Gamecocks).

Even if the quality of play lags behind what American fans are accustomed to in terms of style and execution, games are not without entertainment. To an American who still finds soccer fan culture a novelty, the fan experience is also fun with its singing, chanting, and off-color jabs. Each team is good for a few trick plays per game, the wide receiver reverse being the favorite. Enough good running backs play in the league that fans will usually be treated to a couple of 80-yard breakaway touchdown runs followed by some pretty creative touchdown celebrations. Tackling is generally poor—hence some of the 80-yard runs—but Turkish players are generally strong and a few of them seem especially adept at channeling their Ottoman warrior ancestry and delivering the violent hits football fans enjoy most. Some sort of heated argument or fight is also likely to happen each game, adding interest if not civility.

These fights are a testament both to Turkish emotion and the role of shame and honor within the society. Balıkçı, for example, was ejected from our first play-out match because he lost his temper and fought an opposing player. I later learned that the opposing player had cursed Balıkçı's mother and defending his family's honor required a reaction, something the opponent no doubt understood and took advantage of. Understanding Turkish emotionalism and the concept of honor explains many of the fights one might see in Turkey, from the scuffle over a traffic accident to politicians tussling in Parliament. Also stemming from the concepts of shame and honor embedded within Turkish culture is the absolute refusal of game officials to apologize or back down from error. Granted, nowhere are referees known for their humility and swift self-corrections; they are authorities and must avoid all appearances of weakness or indecision. However, if an egregious mistake is made—everybody in Missouri say "fifth down"—the least that is expected of officials and their supervisors is an admittance of error and a promise to do better next time. Not in Turkey. To admit fault would be to invite shame.

Once, in the wake of an especially poor call—our nose guard took the ball from the quarterback, but the official ruled the quarterback's forward progress had been stopped—I did not get an apology, but an ejection. I was flagged for unsportsmanlike conduct and forced to coach the final two minutes from behind the chain-link fence surrounding the field. The official later told me that he had to maintain his authority, and thus his honor, in front of the players and that my animated protest could not be tolerated any longer. In other games officials made calls that could be said, with only slight exaggeration, to insult the enterprise of human rationality and dignity altogether. False start on the defense. Face-masking penalty on the guy *getting* face-masked. Ejecting a player and making it up that he was smoking on the bench (not entirely improbable, but nevertheless in this case untrue). Talking on a cell phone *during* the game. Issuing a yellow card—in *American* football. No depth of comedy remains unexplored in the realm of Turkish officiating.

All good rules, however, have an exception. And thankfully, the officials in the 2011 championship game overturned one of the worst calls I've ever witnessed, but only after much shaming protest. The game featured the perennial powerhouse Boğaziçi Sultans squaring off against the Gazi Warriors, the only team in the league that paid a player that year. Their quarterback, who flew in from Istanbul each week to play for the Ankara-based squad, was worth every *kuruş* as he orchestrated the best passing game I had seen in the country. Tied at the end of regulation, the game went into overtime where NCAA rules are applied. In the second overtime, the Sultans played offense second and a touchdown would win the championship. The quarterback took a three-step drop and threw a slant to a receiver crossing toward the end zone from the right side. A Warrior defender came over his back and was rightly flagged for pass interference. However, the officials ruled that since the interference took place in the end zone that the Sultans would be credited with a touchdown. The game—and the season!—was over. Boğaziçi fans and players erupted in celebration, while the Gazi contingent fought the ruling like their nickname demanded they should. The field was chaos for at least ten minutes while the referees discussed the call. Eventually the ruling was overturned and Gazi eventually won in the third overtime of what was nearly a six-hour game. The shame of sticking with *that* call on *that* stage proved to be more than the shame of admitting error.

Another interesting facet of Turkish American football is the presence of female officials, a development that is still radical and slow in the American game. The acceptance and encouragement of female officials is all the more curious given the prevailing gender roles within Turkish society. Generally speaking, outside the home Turkey is a man's world, while women rule the domestic roost. In many smaller cities and towns, at certain times of day a visitor will only see men on the street. The wife is at home preparing to serve the husband when he returns home. Women are relegated to the back or upstairs of the mosque for prayers. Most government officials are men. Domestic violence to "keep women in line" is a cultural norm. Women do most all the work around the house, including the grunt work of village farming, while the men drink tea, play backgammon, and complain about politics. It is a man's world. Yet, relative to other regional states, women have also been given incredible opportunity. Women were given the right to vote in 1930, only ten years after women in the United States were granted suffrage and a full fifteen years before those sophisticates in France made such concessions. In 1993, Tansu Çiller became Turkey's first female prime minister. Urban women attend university and work in large numbers. That the TAFL employs female referees marks the sport as a largely urban and western Turkey phenomenon, while also providing a glimpse into a possible egalitarian future of gender in Turkey.

My favorite official in Turkey was the female referee in our game in Izmir against the *Efeler*, or Swashbucklers. She was young and pretty, but that was not the reason she was my favorite. My young and pretty wife was on the sidelines with me (because we were advised that this was not the safest neighborhood for young pretty foreign women, the coaches' wives stayed inside the fence surrounding the field). Rather, I point out that she was young and pretty because she seemed—pardon the chauvinism—too dainty to handle the burly and often angry football players. Had she been like one of the *teyzes* who muscle their way around the open air markets —large, covered, long nose, and a scowl that would turn Bobby Knight to butter—I would have understood possessing the necessary gumption to officiate a football game. Teyzes tell people what to do like it is their patriotic duty. But this gal looked more likely to go out on a date with one of the players than call him for holding. She made one call the entire game, incorrectly calling our wide receiver in bounds when he was clearly out of bounds. She was not the only referee to make a blatant mistake, but she was the only one who ever made a blatant mistake in our team's favor, which is why she is my favorite Turkish referee.

Eventually—sometimes six hours later—the game will end. The teams will line up on the fifty-yard line to shake hands. Winners will celebrate loudly. Dancing may be involved. Losers will quietly walk off the field. Trash will be scattered all over the field, an assortment of water bottles, cups, and athletic tape. After all, to pick it up would take someone else's job away. I'll count uniforms and helmets like a miser, praying we get them all back, not actually believing that we will. We'll eat dinner at a local dive and buy a waffle with ice cream to eat for dessert on the bus. We'll get back on the road for the long trip home. The players, too tired to dance, will put on headphones and drift to sleep as we ride off into the Anatolian sunset. We'll drive all night, stopping for tea and soup and cigarettes, and arrive back home just as Istanbul awakens for another day.

ÇAY BREAK

You've heard of Southern hospitality? Alabama ain't got nothing on Arhavi, pardon the Southern double negative. Charleston might as well be a cold New York morning after another Jets loss. This small town in Turkey's northeast corner, nestled between the Black Sea and the Kaçkar mountains, has more charm than a witchdoctor.

Growing up in South Carolina I am accustomed to southern politeness. I say "yes ma'am" and "mister" to anyone more than a few years older than me. While driving, I wave at people whether I know them or not. I hold doors for people and even ask them how they are doing. But I'm not accustomed to what I experienced in Arhavi. My group of American tourists met some folks one night. We drank tea together the next morning and were invited back for dinner that evening.

But not just any dinner. They threw a party. Lots of fresh river trout and local fondue and a specialty custard dessert. Lots of friends and folk songs and a musician playing their version of a bagpipe.

We drove in the snow to a village just up from town. That morning one girl in our group had mentioned liking Laz Böreği, a famous dessert from the area. So a lady and her mother made it for us. We ate fresh trout from the river that flowed by the restaurant and a lovely concoction called muhlama, which is made of butter, cheese, more butter, more cheese, corn flour, and a little more butter just in case your arteries were not sufficiently clogged. Apparently, that was not enough butter and cheese so they then brought out a second appetizer that was cheese covered in melted butter.

I could hear myself getting fatter.

After dinner we drank tea while sitting around a wood stove, listening to folk music on the bagpipe, singing along, and dancing. When there was not enough room inside to dance properly we moved outside. So there we were, eight American tourists interlocking pinkies in a circle with new friends, dancing in the snow in a village in the middle of nowhere Turkey.

I love my life.

The night ended with a snowball fight and pushing our vehicles across the icy and snowy bridge. We met again for tea in the morning, which included an invitation to stay and to go on a road trip to Georgia for the day. We had to decline, but at the mention of my wife and I having a baby, I was assured a place to stay if we return in the summer. I've visited several times since and have yet to stay in a hotel again.

I wondered where I could go to get that treatment in the United States? I wondered if my name were Ahmet if I would get invited into an American home. If we would dance. If we would throw snowballs and a party.

I've learned something living in Turkey. I've learned what hospitality really looks like. And it's more than waving and smiling and saying "howyadoin'?" I've been the outsider who's been made to feel like an insider. I've been the foreigner made to feel like family.

I decided that when I'm back in the States that I want to practice a more hospitable Southern hospitality. I want to show Arhavi hospitality.

8

TEBOWING

Though his normal position was wide receiver, Onur called dibs on a few carries at running back before the Parslar game. Knowing the Parslar, or Panthers in English, were a first-year team our players were confident we would win by a large margin, thus giving Onur the opportunity to play out of position without worry. Leading by more than sixty points with only minutes left to play, time was drawing nigh to give Onur the ball and an opportunity to score. With the ball around the opponent's 35-yard line I gave Onur the green light to sub in at running back after the ensuing play. Unfortunately for him, a rookie running back ran 35 yards for the touchdown on that play before Onur could enter the game. He would have to settle for running the two-point conversion, which he did happily. As it turned out, Onur was wanting in the game not so much for the clout of scoring a touchdown, as I suspected, as much as for the fun of the touchdown celebration.

Onur ran off tackle on the right side for an easy two points. Then, he dropped to one knee. Onur was Tebowing, flanked by two other Tebowers to his right and left. I dropped to my knees laughing.

The comedy of our Muslim players Tebowing was too much, particularly when I realized that his weeklong insistence on scoring was with this celebration in mind.

Why would Muslim Turks imitate an American evangelical poster-boy?

The answer probably has more to do with pop culture than religion. Tim Tebow's 2011-12 NFL season with the Denver Broncos—his success coupled with his famous prayer posture— generated a worldwide "Tebowing" phenomenon in which people around the world posted photos and videos of themselves Tebowing in various places. With more than 32 million Facebook users in Turkey, good for sixth most in the world, Turks were not going to miss out on this viral craze.

Yet our question, perhaps even our confusion, of Muslim Turks striking the prayer pose of a prominent evangelical Christian reveals our misunderstanding of the role and nature of religion in Turkey, more specifically that of Islam.

Religion is embedded in Turkish culture, its roots firmly planted in monotheism. Abraham, a prophet prominent in the three Great Monotheistic faiths—Judaism, Christianity, and Islam—was from what is now known as Şanlıurfa in southeast Turkey. A large mosque commemorates him there. In Roman times the Jewish diaspora was spread all across the land that is modern Turkey. After the resurrection of Jesus, his followers scattered to these diaspora cities and the early Christian church was born in places like Antioch (Antakya), Galatia (Ankara and its outlying areas), Pontus (the Black Sea coast), Smyrna (Izmir), Ephesus (Efes), and many others. Of course at this time, not all religious belief was monotheistic. Mythology and idolatry dominated the Hellenistic world, a notable example being Artemis of the Ephesians. Early Christianity penetrated these bastions of idolatry, winning converts and fulfilling the great messianic promise that God's salvation was for all peoples, not just for the Jews.

The rise of the Seljuk Turks and their westward expansion in the eleventh century began the slow conversion of Anatolia from Greek-speaking Christianity to Turkish-speaking Islam. In 1453, when Sultan Mehmet II's forces conquered Constantinople—which had become the second incarnation of Rome in the fourth century—the Muslim Ottoman Empire was cemented as a Eurasian power. Conversion to Islam was coerced, undoubtably sometimes by the sword, but other times through economic policies. One town along the Black Sea coast allegedly received its name from repeated attempts to convert the local population via heavy taxation. As the legend goes, the Ottoman empire levied harsher taxes on Christians. Every time a the tax man came to collect, the locals would say "Offf," a common Turkish sigh roughly equivalent to "ugh." The town was among the last to convert and today is known as Of, located in Trabzon province.

The conversion of the region and the transformation into an Islamic society has been prolific. Today, mosques dominate every cityscape, the languid chant of the call to prayer booms from every direction five times per day. "To be Turkish is to be Muslim" is a popular saying and while it is not entirely accurate—I know Turks who are Christians—it captures the spirit of the age. Turkey is most definitely a Muslim nation, with more mosques per capita than most Middle Eastern countries.

With religion so deeply embedded in the culture, religious conversations are neither taboo nor unnatural as might be the case in the post-Christian western world. I am often asked about my religious beliefs, the assumption being that I am Catholic. Upon hearing that I am not Catholic I am seen as Orthodox, generally their only other default frame of reference for Christians. Since tensions exist between Turks and typically Catholic Armenians and typically Orthodox Greeks I generally prefer to not even use the term "Christian." Most of the time "Christian" carries more cultural and political overtones than religious meaning in Turkey, partly due to the historical observation that little separation exists between matters of faith, culture and politics in Islamic cultures. I prefer to simply tell people that I follow Jesus.

Though religion is deeply embedded in Turkish culture and Turkey is a Muslim nation, it does not necessarily mean that all Turks are particularly religious. A quick glance around the street at prayer time affords the opportunity to see that most people simply tune out the minaret's call. Turkish Islam is different than Arabic Islam. To be a Muslim in good standing in Turkey, it seems that all one must do is confess that he is Muslim. Beyond that it is socially acceptable to be as devout or lax as one wishes. In Istanbul, irreligion is not only acceptable, but common, even preferred in some neighborhoods. One friend, within the same conversation, defined himself as both an atheist and a Muslim.

Spend a few hours with our football team and you will soon recognize that football players mostly represented the religiously lax side of the population. Few, if any, attended prayers at the mosque or kept the Ramadan fast. Many of our players ignore the Islamic prohibition of alcohol, frequenting the upscale bar that one of our players opened in the hip Taksim district of Istanbul. It is not that our players are devoid of religious beliefs. Rather, they have syncretized Islam with Turkish liberty and secularism like so many of their countrymen, particularly in the larger cities. Turkish Islam, then, is much different than the western stereotypical understanding of Muslims. For many, identity is found more in education and socioeconomic status than religion.

How did Turkey, the heir of the Ottoman Empire whose Sultan doubled as the Caliph, arrive at a place where one can be both Muslim and an atheist, where almost every religious requirement can be ignored with no seeming consequence? The answer lies in Turkey's most beloved figure, Mustafa Kemal Atatürk. At the founding of modern Turkey, Anatolia was home to multiple ethnic people groups, some with historical ties to religions other than Islam, mostly Christianity. Atatürk, armed with knowledge of the desperate need for unity, embarked on a quest to forge a Turkish national identity that superseded any other loyalties, lest his new nation state be divided up again like their post-WWI fate. Atatürk used nationalistic Islam—that is, tying Islam to Turkishness—as a unifying principle even though he was not particularly religiously devout himself. At the same time Atatürk set up a secular democratic government, the first of its kind in the Muslim world.

And so it was, Turks would be Muslims, but not necessarily in the public square. Education and government would take on European forms. Atatürk changed the alphabetic script from Arabic to Latin. Women's head scarves, a religious symbol, were banned in government offices and state universities.

As the years passed a new religious devotion cropped up in Turkey—*Kemalism*. Kemalists, though they would not outright admit it, pretty much worship Atatürk in admiration of his strongman tactics of both pushing out the foreign invader and of galvanizing Turkey's collective identity. This admiration that has morphed into a cult of personality that remains pervasive both in Istanbul and across Anatolia. They tattoo his signature on their forearms and place a decal of it on their car windows. They might charge you with breaking Article 301—"insulting Turkishness"—if you impugn his name, a crime punishable by prison. To commemorate Atatürk's death, each November 10th at 9:05 a.m.—the precise time of his death—everyone stops for a minute of silence and tribute. Traffic screeches to a halt, even on major highways, as drivers step out of their vehicle to stand at attention. It is at once inspiring and eerie, deeply respectful and kind of creepy. The greatest snapshot of Atatürk's place as a religious figure is a sign that used to stand near the docks in Kadıköy, a secularist haven. It featured a cross for Christianity, a crescent moon for Islam, a Star of David for Judaism, and Atatürk's face for Kemalism. He is the fourth great religion in Turkey, with more adherents than Christianity and Judaism combined.

The last decade, however, has seen something of a resurgence of conservative Islam in Turkey. The ruling Justice and Development Party (AKP), a right-of-center Islamic party, has risen to great power, even to the point of potentially drafting a new constitution. Fifteen years ago you would not have seen very many women donning headscarves in public. Today, approximately half of all women are covered. In some conservative neighborhoods it is not uncommon to see women wearing the full burka, or what one of our players deridingly called "the ninja" outfit. Recent public educational reform legislation allows for religious education for younger children and also makes high school elective courses on the Quran and the life of Muhammad available. These events have caused major concern among some of Turkey's less religiously devout and even led to a fistfight in Parliament when the education reform bill was being discussed. One team leader mentioned to me on more than one occasion that Turkey will be just like Iran in a few years, a prediction I have heard from others. I do not connect his name with that comment as the religio-political climate is such that he could face punishment for those views being published.

Today there are two large streams of religious thought, each with its own tributaries. There is a stream of Turks devoted to Islam. They keep at least some of the religious requirements, such as the Ramadan fast, prohibition against alcohol and pork, head coverings, and prayers at the mosque. Many in this stream vote for the Justice and Development Party. They can usually be recognized by their dress; beanie caps, beards, and prayer beads for men and long coats and headscarves for women. The second stream can also be generally recognized by their dress, most notably the women who leave not only their heads uncovered, but most of their body as well. It is a rather odd circumstance to be on the same bus as a lady in full "ninja" gear and a lady who looks like she just walked off the set of *Pretty Woman*. This second stream, though still claiming Islam, seemingly connects very little of Islam into their daily lives. They are more devoted to the functional gods of money, education, jobs, social networks, and their Turkish identity than to the teachings of the Quran. Many in this stream vote for the Republican People's Party, the AKP's main opposition. Within each stream tributaries exist that are either more or less like the generalizations I have made. It is beyond the scope of this chapter to explore each movement in depth, but it suffices to remark that Turkish religiosity, even within its common Islamic denominator, is far from monolithic.

At this point you may be asking what all this has to do with American football. On the surface not very much. But it does answer our question about why a Muslim would strike the Tebow prayer pose. Religion is not the organizing thread of life and worldview for him, thus it is not important that he would "pray" like an infidel. His life is organized by family, friends, work, and pop culture; none of those things conflict with Tebowing. Striking the Tebow pose was fun and funny, so he did it.

Further, our exploration of the role of religion in Turkey answers our assumptions about why we find American football in Turkey so odd. It's not that we find American football abroad strange in and of itself—we accept the Canadian version, even if their field is a ridiculous 110 yards long. American football in France does not surprise us even though that means the French are voluntarily engaging in something violent (I wonder if they call it Freedom Football rather than American Football). Rather, we find American football in Turkey odd because Turkey is a Muslim nation. When we think of the word *fast*, we think 40-speed, not Ramadan. A head covering is a helmet, not a scarf. Since 9/11 we have tried to understand this foreign religion with 1.5 billion followers, but unfortunately, most of our misinformed stereotypes about Muslims persist. We hear "Muslim" and recall hijacked airplanes, large turbans, riding on camels, and more hijacked airplanes. But when we take a deeper look at Turkey's religious context, our assumptions about a monolithic Islam are broken down. Not all Muslims are terrorists. Not all Muslims hate America. Not even all Muslims are particularly devout to their faith. In fact, we learn that there is nothing inherent in the Turkish religious experience that would prohibit American football from taking root in Turkey. There may be plenty of cultural quirks—their obsession with soccer or their suspicion of the United States of America—that make it unlikely, but they do not necessarily stem from the religious climate.

Turkey's geography does not help dispel any misconceptions. Technically a part of Central Asia, many view Turkey as part of the Middle East. Neither designation clarifies much. Central Asia is about as known and understood an entity to the average American as the offsides call in soccer is to the average fan at Cowboy Stadium. All the countries might as well be known as Obscurestan. The Middle East tag on Turkey carries its own misconceptions, most notably that it is all desert and Arabic and jihad. I was reminded of this misconception while playing golf with some friends one day in South Carolina. A gentleman asked if there were any golf courses in Turkey, to which I replied there is one that I know of. "I bet they got plenty of sand to fill the traps," he responded with a chuckle, obviously pleased with his wit. Never mind the fact that he made a similar comment a month earlier and I told him that much of Turkey was greener than the fairway we stood in. To him, Turkey is Muslim country in the Middle East and that means it is one ginormous sand trap. His is a popular misconception, but I do not blame him. It is hard to filter out reality from years of selective news reports, which is generally the only way most people hear about the region.

Others are less worried about the climate and topography and more focused on our safety, thinking we must be at all times surrounded by jihadists hell-bent on our demise. While I appreciate the concern, I have not met the first jihadist. Rather, my Turkish friends, including the deeply religious ones, deplore terrorism and think themselves morally superior to those who advocate such brute violence. Far from being hostile to my family, the Turks have welcomed us into their homes to eat and drink with them. While on trips they have insisted we stay the night with them instead of paying for a hotel. I have experienced more hospitality in Turkey than I ever have in America. The Turks have a saying that "any guest is God's guest" and so they go overboard to show hospitality to a guest, especially a foreigner, for any good deed done to a guest is as a good deed done unto God. In their belief system they earn both bad marks and good marks for their deeds, sin and *sevap*. They carry equal and opposite value and at the end of their life, they believe, God will add up their account. Those with more *sevap* than sin will enter into heaven, while those with more sin than *sevap* will spend at least some time in hell.

I became acquainted with the over-the-top kindness of Turkish hospitality in Rize province while on a road trip with two American friends. We met an acquaintance for lunch, a man that I had met a few weeks earlier. During lunch he invited us repeatedly to come spend the night in his village home. I politely refused several times, citing an appointment at a university a few hours away in the next province. On the third invitation I accepted on the condition that I could reschedule my appointment, which I was able to do. After lunch we drank tea at a local cafe where we talked about our lives. He mentioned that he had lived in another city for a while and it was there that he spent time in prison for shooting and wounding a man. Not knowing him very well yet it was at this point in the conversation that I began to question my decision to go into the mountains with him. We went anyway.

We stopped by the local school on the way so he could do a little show-and-tell of the Americans to his children and their friends. Soon after we arrived at his mountaintop village home. Tea fields covered the surrounding hills and in the distance was a beautiful view of the snowcapped Kaçkar mountains. I could not help but think that if this real estate was in America it would be worth millions of dollars. In fact, if this had been in America profiteering carpetbaggers would have turned it into a gated golf community long ago. Thankfully, the natural beauty of the area had been preserved, even after the tea farming industry cropped up in the mid-1900s.

Not long after arriving our friend informed us that we were going to go fishing. Just before we left to walk down into the ravine to fish, my friend who had spent time in prison for shooting someone leaned in close to ask, "you're not afraid of guns are you?" Now, I grew up in South Carolina where four-year-olds hunt with rifles and the right to bear arms is the *second* amendment only because some Yankees—who apparently like to talk—thought free speech more important. So I am not afraid of guns. I am, however, scared of people who shoot other people with guns. So, I quickly texted a friend in Istanbul my location in case this situation went south. It turned out that the gun was for our protection from the wild boars and bears known to roam the woods. We made it to the creek and our friend caught baby trout with his bare hands like he was Bear Grylls. On the walk back up the hillside I was keeping my eyes squarely on the narrow path through the tea field when I heard *BANG BANG BANG.* Our friend, bringing up the rear, was firing out over the valley and obviously tickled that he was able to startle us with the shots. We each took turns firing the .38 caliber revolver, relieved we were not being shot with it and hoping we had not accidentally broken the Sixth Commandment somewhere on the other side of the valley.

That night his wife prepared a feast for us. We ate the trout, which we knew were fresh by the red dots on them. That and the fact that we saw our friend catch them with his bare hands. She also prepared chicken, rice, bread, salad, and a heavenly mixture of cornmeal, butter, and cheese called *muhlama.* After dinner she brought out fresh hazelnuts to snack on. After that, popcorn. Later came a king's portion of fruit, including kiwis from their garden. At 11:00 p.m. and stuffed to the brim I was taken aback at the words that came from my friend's mouth. "You know what we need? Some baked potatoes." So they threw some potatoes into the wood oven in their living room, which also served as the only heat source in the house, and we ate plain baked potatoes for a midnight snack.

During the course of the evening we talked of religion much as it is a natural conversation topic. They told me what they believed and I told them what I believed. I referenced our Bible several times and read from a Turkish version I keep on my phone. The next day this couple remarked to us that our lives were much better than theirs. I did not understand. I thought their lives were great. They lived atop a mountain, grew all their own food, grew tea as a cash crop, and seemed to have a happy family. Why were our lives so much better? I then realized they were talking about our moral lives. So I asked why and they gave two reasons. First, we knew our Holy Book. We knew where things were in it. Second, we brushed our teeth twice a day. It was then that I learned the keys to morality: know your Book and personal hygiene!

I tell this story because it is my favorite story about Turkish hospitality. They fed us more food than we ever wanted. They allowed us—basically strangers—to stay in their home. And some of what occurred is bafflingly funny. All the fun and food was designed to treat us as guests of God. It was their way of loving us and welcoming the foreigner to their country. And at some level, it was their way of earning sevap. The more food we ate, the more sevap they earned. The baked potatoes tipped both their scales (of sin and sevap) and mine (of pounds and kilograms).

We said at the beginning of the book that Turkey was odd because it is different than what one would expect. Nowhere is the gap between our Western expectations and the reality of Turkey seen more clearly than the subject of religion. We expect ultraconservative theocracy from an Islamic state, but instead we find secular democracy. We expect burka-covered women, but we find miniskirts. We expect jihad, but we find baked potatoes at midnight. And as soon as we get comfortable with these new expectations we make new discoveries. Some political parties are very much religiously motivated and religion is not barred from the public square. Half of the women cover their heads for religious reasons and some don the full burka. Many people are vehemently opposed to other religions and to the government of the United States of America on religious and political grounds. The lesson, as always, is we must be very careful with our expectations.

The football team taught me that Turkish Islam is not monolithic. The overwhelming majority of our players were living proof that many Turks are more committed to secularism than classical Islam. Religion was not an organizing thread in their lives. But other players represented a much more devout stream of Turks, those that prayed in the mosque and kept the Ramadan fast. Religion tied them to their family, their past, and their god. For example, Ercan was a leading defensive lineman and he unlocked his neighborhood mosque some mornings. And lest the religiously devout be mistakenly thought of as piously boring, I should note that Ercan was one of our most boisterous comedians and practical jokesters. He is an animated storyteller who used his hands, feet, and belly to spin a good yarn. The Stallions team included both mosque-goers and Tebowers, illustrating that the religious fabric of Turkey is very complex.

In some respects, this texture is very beautiful. A measure of religious freedom exists in Turkey. Opportunities are available for women in Turkey that are not found in other religiously strict nations. People are allowed, to some extent, to make their own choices. Citizens of varying degrees of devout religiosity unite around a common patriotism. Yet, not all is beautiful. Religious difference is often a spark for turmoil and in the summer of 2013 the multifaceted nature of Turkey's national religion resulted in street violence and protest.

9

THE FIERY BLAZE IN TAKSIM

In the wee morning hours of May 31, 2013 my sixteen-month-old son woke up screaming and inconsolable, an anomaly for my normally well-sleeping kid. Likely, separation anxiety and the influx of out-of-town guests we had in and out of our apartment at the time got the best of him. Or perhaps he sensed the mood of the nation and knew a riot, or something like it, was afoot. I got up to soothe my son and to try my best to keep him quiet so as not to disturb our newly arrived, jet-lagging friends from their slumber. Since he let forth bloodcurdling shrieks each time I tried to lay him back down in bed, I was left to stay up rocking him, and I logged onto Facebook on my phone to pass the time. There, I discovered the unrest that would spread across the country over the ensuing weeks and mark the summer of 2013 as one of protest and resistance. My Facebook news feed was almost entirely filled with updates, rants, pleas, and declarations about a burgeoning protest movement in the heart of Istanbul, Taksim Square. I followed the story via Facebook updates from football players as protestors rallied from all corners of the city toward Taksim. I watched a live-stream video feed as thousands walked across the Bosphorus Bridge as day broke. Slogans like "Everywhere Taksim, Everywhere Resistance" and hashtags such as #ResistGeziPark took over social media. And as the sun rose early that spring morning, it seemed as if a "Turkish Spring" was also rising, a new day in the Turkish public square.

Like forest fires that start with just a small spark, the protests that swept the nation began humbly enough. A group of environmentalists gathered in Taksim's Gezi Park, one of the last remnants of green space left in the heart of the city, to protest the government's decision to turn the park into a shopping mall fashioned after the old Ottoman military barracks that once stood in that space. Protestors staged a sit-in for three days until state police began to crack down on them in an effort to force protestors to leave ahead of bulldozers moving in. Using social media outlets like Facebook and Twitter, environmentalist protestors called for more people to join the sit-in, an invitation many heeded. In the early hours of May 31, police moved in to Gezi Park firing water cannons, tear gas, and pepper spray into the crowds, a show of force protestors, observers, and, later, even the government would deem excessive. The "woman in red" became the iconic image of the early protests, a photograph showing a young Turkish lady in a red sundress getting blasted at pointblank range with pepper spray by a police officer.

While Gezi Park remained the center of the resistance over the next month, environmental issues gave way to larger political concerns as the secular, progressive, Westward-looking segment of the population found occasion to voice its discontent with the Islamic-leaning ruling party and prime minister Recep Tayyıp Erdoğan. Several issues rose to the forefront for the secularists, each just a harbinger of long-held suspicions and fears. Recently, the government had banned alcohol sales from shops between the hours of 10:00 p.m. and 6:00 a.m., banned all advertising for alcohol, and barred any shop selling alcohol from opening within 100 meters of schools and mosques. The educational system had also been revised, introducing religious education to students at a younger age and providing extra funding for religious schools. Issues regarding freedom of the press, free speech, and freedom to assemble were also raised, as well as the government's actions to undermine the power of the Turkish army, long the arm of enforcement for Turkish secularism.

Other recent events and actions also primed the pump for protest. The acronym T.C.—representing *Türkiye Cumhuriyeti*, translated as *Republic of Turkey*—was removed from the name and signage of a large government bank and the ministry of health, a slap to the face of Turkish patriotism. The government imposed, at various times, Internet restrictions, including blocking the popular blogging website, Blogger.com. Construction on a controversial large 57,000-square-meter mosque to be built atop one of Istanbul's highest hills began. The prime minister spoke out against public displays of affection, to which dozens of protestors took to Ankara's subway to protest by kissing. I can imagine a young, lovestruck Ahmet telling his beloved Fatma, *"But this is important. We must protest. We must make out on the subway!"*

More serious was how the Turkish populace viewed the government's policy on neighboring Syria's civil war. Erdoğan and Syrian president Bashar al-Assad, who once vacationed together with their families in the south of Turkey, became at odds with one another, Erdoğan allying himself with the West in a commitment to see Assad's regime overthrown. Turkish public opinion was not sided with regime change and when 52 people were killed and 140 wounded in twin car bomb attacks in Reyhanlı along the Syrian border, the government's Syrian policy was blamed.

So when the police moved into Gezi Park in late May 2013, saving a few trees and opposing yet another Istanbul shopping mall were not the only issues at play. Police action at Gezi Park was the proverbial straw placed not so gently on the camel's back. This particular event simply gave roughly half of the population an opportunity to resist what they saw as an increasingly Islamist and authoritarian government encroaching on their rather secular world.

Erdoğan and the ruling Justice and Development Party (AKP)

were not without large support. The AKP won recent elections with fifty percent of the vote, while the opposition was splintered into multiple disagreeing factions. Erdoğan held several large rallies during the protests to display the widespread support he had garnered across the nation. From the AKP's viewpoint they were acting in the interest of the nation's majority to help raise up a pious generation of youth, educated in the people's chosen religion and free from the snares of alcohol. The removal of "T.C." from some signage represented the privatization of banks and hospitals. Syrian rebels, not the Turkish government, were responsible for the Reyhanlı attack, they argued. And with all due respect to love, the subway is probably not the most appropriate place for young lovers to make out.

With all these political issues at play, the stage was set for dramatic theater, which is exactly what unfolded over the course of June 2013. Ignited when police tried to force Gezi Park protestors out of the park, the resistance spread throughout the city and all over the country, with solidarity protests held in Izmir, Ankara, and even as far away as Toronto. Scenes broadcast all over the world were brutal. Civilians blasted by water cannons. Riot police firing pellets and tear gas into crowds. Protesters ripping up bricks from the road and hurling them at police. Fires. Overturned police vehicles. Graffiti. Neither side seemed completely innocent and a little "chicken or the egg" tension existed as to who escalated the chaos.

Even in the midst of such widespread mayhem and the warzone-like images that emerged online and on television, the amazing thing to me was how peaceful the protests remained. This statement is not to minimize the admitted violence that occurred—real people were injured and abused. The city was indeed in upheaval for a season. But, unlike the Arab Spring protest movements, particularly the revolution in Egypt, Turkey never experienced bloody days where hundreds of citizens were murdered. In fact, ordinary citizens who never ventured out to the hotspot protest areas peacefully protested by flickering their lights on and off and banging on pots and pans at 9:00 p.m. each evening. After the initial days of confrontation, the scene in Taksim became like a festival during the days. Musicians performed, poets read their latest works, and a makeshift library was erected. Protestors stayed active by doing yoga in the park, while others snacked on fresh watermelon. Many protestors would work their jobs by day and return to Taksim to protest by night. Occasionally, however, the day festival would turn into a night fight, as clashes with the police broke out. But still, the violence—as bad as it was—rarely escalated to bloodshed, a mark in favor of Turkey's march toward modernity.

The public face of the protest movement was given to the intellectual and creative class that spurred the movement on social media with wit and cleverness. Most of our football team belong to this class to one degree or another. They represent a largely middle-to-upper class, university educated, English-speaking, internationally focused, well-traveled population segment. They won the battle in the international press with their liberalism and their humor. In response to the incessant pepper spray, they resisted police by throwing red chili peppers at them. They incorporated lines from popular old Turkish movies into Internet memes. When Erdoğan referred, with snide condescension, to the protestors as "*birkaç çapulcu*"—a few looters or riffraff—protestors turned the phrase into a badge of honor, inserting *çapulcu* as an honorific in front of their names on Facebook. "Çapulling" became a verb meaning to stand up for one's rights and "Everyday I'm Çapulling," a video spoof of the pop song "Everyday I'm Shuffling," went viral around the world. On one of the opening nights of protest, when the unrest was at its height, CNN International covered the events live, showing the fiery blaze in Taksim and all the back-and-forth fighting between police and protesters. At the same time, CNN TÜRK broadcast a documentary about penguins, a choice that reinforced widely held beliefs about the government's control of media outlets. Thus, penguins became one of the enduring icons of the protest movement, being featured in countless political cartoons and Internet memes. A few days later, a Turkish actor and political activist was a guest on CNN TÜRK to discuss the unfolding events. He wore a penguin t-shirt.

97

Eventually, protesters were evacuated and barred from Gezi Park and concessions were made to the protesters, including a temporary postponement of Gezi Park redevelopment plans and a promise that future development plans would not be made without public consultation and referendum. The intensity of the protests waned and eventually Istanbul life returned to normal, though the political landscape was not left unchanged and the kindling of widespread protests remains just a spark away from ignition.

So how does American football explain the 2013 summer protest movement? Directly, it does not. But indirectly, the American football subculture generally represents a larger slice of Turkey's population devoted to Atatürk's secular ideal, that has little to no formal allegiance to religious Islam, and outright opposes political Islam. They have affinity for the West as evidenced by their love of American football and the culture that accompanies the sport. They are university educated, relatively wealthy, and are the likely heirs of Turkey's business and creative enterprises, which are key culture-shaping sectors of any society. The continual rise in popularity of the sport shows that the westward-leaning secularists are not disappearing from Turkey, particularly from the cities, even as popular support for an Islamist-leaning party swells around the country, particularly in the rural areas.

This conflict is not likely to dissipate.

10

Throwing A Smeagol Tantrum

Nicknames were often bestowed on Stallions players, often because veteran players could not remember the names of newcomers. Or perhaps it was due to the fact that if you called out "Ahmet" or "Muhammad," twelve guys are likely to answer. Elvis got his name because he had sideburns and loved to sing, though not well. One of his favorite tunes was Katie Perry's "I kissed a girl and I liked it," not exactly a tribute to Graceland and a dubious claim. To some players Elvis also went by Smealgol, the Stoor Hobbit that became Gollum in Tolkien's *The Hobbit*, because of his Middle Earthian appearance. He hated the nickname, but allowed Onur to use it, saying, "only my prez can call me that," referring to Onur's role as team president.

In a game against the Gazi Warriors, during the Coach Tim era, Elvis would go down in Stallions lore, though not for desirable reasons. Gazi had a reputation for being the dirtiest team in the league, tough like street kids, rough like criminals. They ran double tight-end sets before Belichick made it cool, never passed, and ran it down your throat and right through you. This team played like its name, *Gazi*, which means *warrior*.

At some point during the game, Elvis starts yelling—not singing —and stomps to the sideline irate, telling Coach Tim very emotionally and in perfect English, "there are sons of bitches on field!" He then tried to kick a water bottle, but struck out after three misses. He threw both the water bottle and himself to the ground, throwing a tantrum. Unfortunately for him, sixty players from the Ankara Cats, waiting to play the nightcap, were perched behind the bench and laughing hysterically. A few Stallions players joined their guffaw.

Why did Elvis turn the football field into the *Heartbreak Hotel*? What had him all shook up? What happened that was so terrible? Well, apparently, a Gazi player told him he was going to kill him on the next snap. And…(waiting….silence…chirping) oh, that's it. He did not say anything else. That, apparently, was enough to send Elvis to a tantrum.

Elvis is a perfect example of how emotional Turks can be, not uncommon for Mediterranean peoples. Granted, most Turks would not throw a Smeagol tantrum at such a benign threat, but their sleeves wear emotions like a Hilfiger label. Earlier, I mentioned the time the normally jovial Balıkçı got angrier than a carp out of water when an opponent insulted his mother. He was also ejected from several other games that season for referee-related rage (to which I will quote Chris Rock, "I'm not saying it's right, but I understand"). Batur, the Audi-driving, celebrity-dating running back, was also prone to emotional outbursts. After cursing the referees to earn an early exit from our play-out game in Ankara, he slung his helmet toward the graying sky as he approached the sideline, a cardinal sin against all that is decent in sports. In our final game a year later, he joined Saygun in the tirade at Coach Jay and me on the sidelines for suspending them for the first half.

Of course, emotions often run hot on the football field, whether that field is in Turkey or the Texas or anywhere. Competition breeds emotional fire. But I find it interesting that Turks often *self-describe* themselves as emotional and instances such as these from the football world serve to highlight what goes on in the broader culture.

A daily commute will often reveal the emotionality of Turks. For instance, I once just missed taking a door off of a car in the opposite lane because the driver flung it open just as I was passing in order to get out and pick a fight with the driver ahead of him. Roadside fights are not uncommon, though they normally take on the flavor of an NBA fight, which is to say there is a lot of pushing and yelling and "hold me back!" but very little actual fighting. One of my Turkish teachers, a calm and well-mannered lady in the classroom, informed us that every morning on the drive to school she screams and curses at other drivers the entire time. Cheap therapy, she calls it. She then settles in with a hot cup of tea, patiently teaching Turkish to a group of foreigners who do the equivalent of a five-car pileup to the Turkish language.

Jealousy is another emotion often expressed in relationships, most notably, if not a tad stereotypically, among women. I have more than one friend who has to be careful whom she visits in her neighborhood, and how often, so as not to offend other friends, lest they think she likes the other friends more. An ownership quality to relationships seems to be in play—"she's *my* friend." Our neighbor has told us on more than one occasion after giving us some fruit or other edibles not to tell our other neighbor lady because she would be jealous.

Violating particular relational and social norms can result in the harsh emotional response of *kusmek*, a cultural phenomenon akin to exclaiming, "*I'm never talking to you again!*" To *kus* someone is to cut off all communication for a period of time, maybe forever. Family members *kus* one another, as do friends or colleagues. Depending on the offense the relationship may be restored in a variety of ways. For something small the offending party need only to show up and spend some time with the offended, perhaps offering an apology. Other times a mediator is necessary, someone who can gather both individuals and talk out a peaceful solution. One friend uses his father as a mediator when he and his sister are *kusmek*. An American friend learned that communicating by phone or text message is not acceptable. Thinking as a Westerner, he tried to break the ice with some communication from a distance to see how his friend would respond. When he responded coldly, my friend took it that they needed more time. When they discussed it later, my friend mentioned the cold text messages, but the Turk simply responded that my friend knew where he worked and should have come to see him. A few days later, the American saw that same friend and another Turk make up after being *kusmek*. Having not spoken for months, they met and talked about everything under the sun except the issue that caused the problem, and afterward he declared to my friend that they had "made peace." The peace came not from talking through the problem and hammering out a solution, but from being together. This solution, of course, makes no sense to me, but it makes perfect sense within the collectivistic and relational Turkish culture. From my experience, if you have ever lived as a middle school girl you are more likely to understand *kusmek*.

Not all of the emotional expressions of Turks are negative. Like other hot weather Mediterranean peoples, such as Greeks, Italians, and Spaniards, Turks are a lively bunch who know how to have fun. They are fantastic storytellers, animated and full of laughter. Engagements, weddings, departure for military duty, and circumcisions are cause for big parties, complete with large meals, fireworks, dancing and car processionals that feature a soundtrack of unceasing car horns, loud music, and gunshots. I'll never forget, just a few weeks after arriving, looking out our apartment window to see a car decorated in Turkish flags and a man hanging out the passenger-side window firing a pistol. I quipped to my wife, "well, either we just witnessed our first wedding or our first drive-by," not fully convinced of either, later learning it was a military send-off party. And if you thought I just sneaked circumcision into the list of celebrations above just to see if you were paying attention, you were wrong; the event is an important rite of passage. It is still strange to me to see banquet halls advertise their circumcision services, but it makes more sense when you realize how they "celebrate," the quotation marks inserted out of sympathy for the young lad in question. When a boy comes of age—somewhere between five and twelve years old—he is dressed as a prince, paraded around town, given a big party and gifts, and then, um, well, snipped. I'm not so sure the party and the prince outfit are worth it.

My favorite expression of Turkish emotion is dancing, as it expresses joy and fun and togetherness like few other customs, for rarely does one dance alone. Many folk dances are found across Turkey, my favorite being the *horon*, a Black Sea regional rendition. To the music of the *tulum*, a bagpipe only slightly different than the Scottish version, or the *kemençe*, fiddle-like in appearance and sound, dancers gather in a circle, interlock their pinkies and slow clog in a counter-clockwise direction. It was the *horon* that we danced in the mountain snow that strange and fun night just outside the little town of Arhavi.

The Stallions players are more than willing to get down with the dancing. Like the bus trip to Mersin, the shuttle van our team ran from campus to the city center often doubled as a disco, though thankfully less sketchy than many Istanbul discos. My friend, Kerim, liked to dance to a certain techno song, which had one lyric sporadically repeated, "Barbara Streisand." The song and the dance were absurd, which only heightened the hilarity of it all. We, thankfully, have several of these dances on video, such as players "Apache" dancing on the escalator of a ritzy mall, booty dancing with each other after a game, or, most recently, a Harlem Shake rendition, which featured one player dancing in his boxers, jersey, helmet, and a smile. Not only can Turks produce fine carpets, but they also know how to cut a rug.

Displays of mass emotion are also common, such as political protests or soccer championship celebrations. After Galatasaray won the 2012 Super League championship, fans flooded Taksim Square to celebrate wildly. Some particularly excited youth climbed the Republic Monument, hanging on with one hand and waving a flag with the other. Countless others fired guns in celebration. Championship rioters in Chicago and Los Angeles would be proud, though I failed to notice any cars set on fire, representing America's clear edge when it comes to senseless acts of celebration.

More seriously, Turkish-Kurdish tensions sometimes lead to mass emotion in the form of ugly, politically motivated riots. In early 2013, a Kurdish political party held a rally in Samsun, but it was cut short by angry locals who decided that hurling large stones at the rally was the best way to disagree. The Kurdish Question is a source of much conflict and has been Turkey's Achilles heel for the last three decades. Though most Americans associate terrorism almost solely with Al Qaeda, most terrorist attacks in Turkey come by the hands— and Molotov cocktails—of the Kurdistan Workers Party, known colloquially as the PKK. A month into our life in Turkey a mobile police station was attacked by bomb in Taksim, the center of European Istanbul and an area we passed three times per week going to our language school. Seven months later another mobile police station was attacked, this time by a bomb on the back of a moped. We've also read in newspapers of a public bus set on fire by a Molotov cocktail, though, thankfully, emptied of its passengers first. The PKK, headquartered in the predominately Kurdish southeast of Turkey, claimed responsibility for all of these acts. They have been fighting for a separate Kurdish state since the 1970s.

Naming these events is not to suggest that only the Kurds are guilty, but rather that the PKK's actions are generally more visible and a greater threat to the security of civilian bystanders. Governments tend to have the luxury of hiding their more unsavory acts. A more serious and academic analysis of the Kurdish Problem should be left to those more expert than I, but I believe a general truism of human conflict holds water here: neither side is innocent and both sides have suffered. This is the type of conflict that cannot be resolved without the forgiveness that is impossible without the shedding of blood, and I'm not talking about war.

Though tensions run canyon deep between Turks and Kurds, they are generally able to separate the person from the People. That is, a Turk may have strong, passionate views about the Kurdish movement in the abstract and perhaps even hold some stereotypical prejudices against Kurds as a group, but he may be friends with a specific Kurdish person in real life. I observed this circumstance on our football team, as Turks and Kurds played together, and I've seen it in my neighborhood, where a Turk and a Kurd may drink tea as friends.

Separating the person from the People is also a general principle for how many view Americans. One taxi driver waxed philosophical on the Turkish position. Turks like Americans, but not the United States as represented by its government. That is, Turks like the specific Americans that they have met, but do not like George Bush, who they see as a murderer for the Iraq War. The subject of American politics comes up often in conversations with anyone older than 30. Before moving into our new neighborhood I visited a local market to make conversation. The store owner asked three questions within the first minute of conversation: *Do you like Bush or Obama?*, *What do you think of Israel?*, and *Do you like war?*, his assumption being that I was an Israel-supporting bloodhound like he perceived Bush to be. I answered in turn, *George Washington*, *I don't know about Israel*, and *I don't like war*. I answered this way not because I am void of political opinions, but because I had no interest in arguing the finer points of geopolitics when my Turkish ability was the equivalent of a two-year old talking under water. (Though now that my Turkish ability has graduated to a-four-year-old-with-a-mouthful-of-Gobstoppers level, I'm happy to engage in a little rhetorical sparring.)

Not only do Turks like the specific Americans they have met, but they like much of American culture. American films and television dominate the viewing habits of young Turks, *How I Met Your Mother* anecdotally being the most popular sitcom. American films are shown in theaters in American-style malls whose food courts feature McDonald's, Burger King, Pizza Hut, and Popeye's. I find it most unfortunate that Popeyes is the Cajun chicken and biscuit representative in Turkey rather than my much beloved Bojangles'; and it is almost criminal that Chick-Fil-A has not joined Turkey's fast food craze (the Muslim government here does realize that "the Christian chicken" spiel is just a joke, right?). More than 450 Burger King franchises are operating countrywide and I feel like I've eaten at half of them with our football players who like to take advantage of getting a second combo meal for just a few extra lira. I would argue a quarter of our offensive line's combined kilograms can be traced to Whoppers. The fact that our American football team and league exist in Turkey is a tribute to the Turks' acceptance of some aspects of American culture.

Turks also like to visit America and, in some cases, move there. Large Turkish populations reside in New Jersey, Washington D.C., Houston, and Raleigh, with smaller populations scattered throughout the country. Even my Turkish friends who have never visited America have many impressions of our land, many thinking Texas is a lawless jungle of unruliness, which may be true, and that Miami is an exotic paradise like heaven, only without the virgins, which is part of the appeal I suspect. Some wealthy Turks plan vacations to the United States that just so happen to coincide with their baby's due date, a happy coincidence I am sure. The prenatal tourism is precipitated by the generous bestowal of American citizenship, and thus a blue passport that can open up national borders and economic doors, on all babies born on American soil. Turks, then, are shocked when I tell them that my son, born in Turkey, was not given Turkish citizenship because neither I nor my wife are Turkish. I feign vexation at the injustice that we accept Turks, but they do not accept us, but inside I know the situation is just as well as it is because he will not have to perform mandatory military service after university and perhaps be thrown into the middle of the Turkish-Kurdish conflict mentioned above.

With my own blue passport and my Southern twanged Turkish, I have experienced nothing but kindness and love living in Turkey. Perhaps some expatriates experience prejudice simply for hailing from the same country as George W. Bush, but I am not among their number. The Stallions accepted Coach Jay and me and our families into their circles with a traditional kiss to the cheek and a smile on their face. Twice we had American cultural exchange students come and play for our team for a semester and those guys were accepted in their neighborhoods and loved on the team. That they could score touchdowns certainly did not hurt their cause.

Yet, for all this acceptance of American people and American culture, there is still overwhelming negative public opinion of the United States of America as a political entity. Some anti-Americanism is no doubt fueled by a "hate the guy at the top" mentality. In many cases the United States, seen as the world's sole superpower, is not liked simply because it is the world's sole superpower. It's a similar phenomenon as football fans irrationally hating Tom Brady because he is the NFL's best quarterback, has won a lot of games and Super Bowls, and is married to the world's highest-paid supermodel. If you want to hate Brady because he endorsed male UGG boots, you'll get no argument from me, but do not hate him because he is what you wish you were. Enjoy it. In the end, however, we tend to be against that which we envy and I think this is what drives at least part of anti-Americanism worldwide.

More so, global anti-Americanism is driven by opposition to American foreign policy, especially the wars in Afghanistan and Iraq. This opposition is also found in Turkey. But there seems to be something else in Turkey driving anti-Americanism in the abstract. In an opinion piece for the Turkish newspaper *Today's Zaman*, Ömer Taşpınar advances the position that American foreign policy is the object of Turkish anti-Americanism, but not its root cause. Rather, its roots lie in the Turkish identity crisis. Taşpınar grounds this claim in the observation that Turkish public opinion about America does not fluctuate as American foreign policy changes. For instance, President Bush was not well liked in Turkey, but President Obama, because he visited Istanbul, is. But public opinion did not change for the better when Obama took office. Turkish-American relations hit a low in 2010 with the flotilla incident and concerns over Israeli relations, but soared in 2012. Taşpınar noted that negative public opinion of America did not really change during that time. Why?

Taşpınar posited that Turkey's anti-Americanism is a reaction to its own identity problems, not American foreign policy *per se*. Conspiracy theories, which are as at-home in Turkey as kebabs, tea, and mosques, drive Turkish anti-Americanism. The first conspiracy theory is that the United States is involved in clandestine operations to help create an independent Kurdish state, a threat to Turkish national identity. The second conspiracy theory is that the United States is in the tank for using Turkey to propagate a moderate Islam in the Middle East, a threat to Turkish secular identity. Add U.S. support for Israel to the mix and Turkish religious identity is threatened as well. And do not forget the leftover communists who still begrudge the Cold War and recently suicide-bombed the American embassy in Ankara. Collective Turkish anti-Americanism makes sense when these theories and fears are added to the equation.

Speaking of conspiracy theories, one of the most widespread theories is about the role and influence of Fethuallah Gülen, a self-imposed political exile now living in Pennsylvania. Gülen is an author, educator, and Muslim theologian. He is an advocate of moderate Islam and runs the largest network of charter schools in the United States, operating under various names: Cosmos Foundation, Harmony Schools, and Rainbow Turkish House. The word on the Turkish street is that he is also a political godfather, pulling strings in both the American and Turkish political arenas. I've been told more than once that the White House has a red phone that Gülen calls to give a directive to Obama who then relays the order to the Turkish prime minister. In this scenario, Gülen is Commissioner Gordon to President Obama's Batman. To extend the analogy Joe Biden is obviously Robin with his sidekick status and foul language; George Bush and his cowboy hat make him the Mad Hatter; Nancy Pelosi's face makes a perfect Joker; and Ron Paul is the Riddler for obvious reasons. Hillary Clinton makes the most sense for Catwoman, but the thought of her in that tight black suit is scarier than a nuclear-armed Iran, so I'm nominating South Carolina governor Nikki Haley for the role. Back to Gülen, the mystery surrounding his role and influence in Turkish politics at home and abroad breeds such conspiracy theories in a country where fear is sometimes the dominating emotion.

I have noticed four types of fear lay their grip on Turkey: political, ethnic, authoritarian and spiritual. The political fear is that the government could fall victim to another *coup d'état*, the republic having experienced four coups in 1960, 1971, 1980, and 1993. Turkey, being a relatively young nation in its latest republican incarnation—the modern state was only founded in 1923—has not yet planted deep roots on the world stage, and shallow rooted trees make easy targets for strong winds. Turkey is also geographically situated in an area of the world where governmental upheaval is common, especially with the recent Arab Spring and its associated regime changes. As I type, a revolution is underway in Syria and it has spilled over into Turkey on several occasions, spilling Turkish blood each time. Turkey is also home to a number of different minority people groups—Kurds, Zazas, Lazuri, Hemşin, and Circassian just to name a few—and the fear of a fractured republic along ethnic lines looms heavy in the political air. Whether it be a split society or a splinter state with new borders, Turks fear ethnic minorities being manipulated—by outsiders or insiders—for political gain. This idea leads to suspicion of outsiders, who are often viewed as intelligence agents intent on destroying the country even if he is simply coaching American football and the closest thing to spying he ever did was scout an opposing team. Hence the suspicion of Baba Zane as an agent. This fear also leads to suspicion of insiders who are seen to be promoting an ethnic minority as a rival to Turkish identity.

The ethnic fear is not a fear of ethnic minorities, but rather ethnic minorities fearing being singled out. Atatürk set about a massive unification project, the basis of which was Turkish national identity and Islam. This project was necessitated by the fact of the many different ethnic groups that lived in Anatolia. Most groups assimilated to one degree or another, but the ones that resisted were dealt with in harsh manner, the violence against the Kurds and Armenians being exhibits A and B. Thus, some of ethnic minority decent shy away from acknowledging their heritage, or even take an ultranationalist political stance. A Turkish man of Crimean Tatar descent once said, "We [Tatars] are more Turkish than the Turks!". It is entirely possible to be friends with someone for months before he would admit he was Kurdish or Hemşin. Until a few years ago it was illegal to speak Kurdish in public, which goes to show that some of the ethnic fear is not unfounded. However, with the relaxation of minority language laws, some of this fear has subsided, but undoing eighty years of assimilation policies will take generations, not years.

Authoritarian fear is just what it seems. Individuals often fear the authority figures in their lives, most notably the man of the house. Husbands and fathers are feared by wives and sons, often with good reason. According to an April 17, 2013 Hurriyet Daily News article, more than a third of Turkish men find domestic violence "occasionally necessary." One night I was riding in the car with a friend in his early twenties. He is normally a happy, outgoing, confident, and fun young man. When his father called to question his whereabouts, he turned into a nervous eight-year-old boy. His female companion in the back seat noticed and asked him about it, no doubt a source of embarrassment for him. Still, his fear of his father was more than his fear of projecting a weak image in front of this young lady.

In conversations with some football players, the role of authoritarian fear in Turkish thought became clearer, but in an odd way. Several players at various times remarked about their admiration of Adolf Hitler as a leader, a notion that causes automatic shock to American ears. They were quick to note that his crimes were evil, but they admired his ability to gather so many followers and dictate his wishes to a nation. Hitler's authoritarian rule was upheld as a virtue because the one who is feared is the one who leads. Turkey's national hero, Atatürk, also ruled with a hard authoritarianism, but without the level of Hitler's brutality. He also is revered for his ability to gather followers and lead a nation. In hindsight, my biggest mistake in coaching the Stallions was not establishing and maintaining authoritarian fear from the first whistle. I sought to make friends on the team at the same time as coaching it effectively, a worthy, but ultimately unhelpful, approach. If players fear you, they respect you, but once the fear is gone oftentimes the respect goes, too. Once respect is gone, you end up with screaming matches on the sidelines with Batur and Saygun. If you ever plan on coaching anything in

Turkey, I recommend bringing your iron fist.

The third fear is spiritual. Turks have an acute awareness of the unseen spiritual world and fear what these spirits or forces can do to them. The most obvious spiritual fear is that the Evil Eye will curse them, their family, their home or business or possessions. To ward off such fear, Turks place the *nazar* charm on everything. Babies, buildings, cars, jewelry and thresholds are all decorated with the charm. A neighbor would often call my baby son ugly so that the Evil Eye would not curse him. She meant he was cute, but to say so would have invited a curse from the jealous force. Another time my son fell down outside and an older lady suggested that he fell down because other kids had invoked a curse on him. *Jinn* is the name given to the spiritual forces at work in the world that can cause a number of problems, according to custom. Another way to ward off the ill intent of the jinn is to say or write "maşallah." Literally, it means "praise," but it is used as a verbal or written charm against evil forces in the same way as the *nazar* bead. The word is seen written on taxis, busses, and cars all over the country and invoked when giving or receiving praise.

Some superstitions are not born out of spiritual fear, but are simply folklore. One such superstition is that sitting on cold surfaces, particularly stone, will cause infertility or other health problems. Thus, women will place a small strip of newspaper on stone or concrete surfaces in order to sit down on them. It remains unclear to me exactly what an inch-wide strip of recycled paper does to protect the reproductive system of a woman. Another superstition is fear of the wind, which, according to some, can cause injury of even death. Fear of wind explains why windows are closed on the overcrowded bus in July or why babies are dressed for the arctic in the middle of summer. One football player was confused as to what caused his neck injury, remarking to me, "I don't understand coach, I wasn't even out in the wind." This same player also once informed me that he could not wear our team practice jersey because he was allergic to the color black. At this point it would be easy to have a snobbishly good chuckle at these silly superstitions, if it were not for the fact we have our own superstitions in America. Cross your fingers. Don't go outside with wet hair or you'll get sick. Don't pick up a penny if it's tails side up. Knock on wood. You get the point. We are also superstitious, even if it is lighthearted. Highlighting the Turkish superstitions are not meant to belittle, but to explain what any visitor would likely notice and wonder about.

Çay Break

My friends and I had just finished rafting the Fırtına river just outside the sleepy town of Ardeşen along Turkey's Black Sea coast. The water level was low and the temperature lower this fall afternoon. We went back to the rafting company's restaurant to eat lunch. After lunch, Ibo, my friend and the owner of the restaurant, invited us to stay the night in his mountain neighborhood.

I politely declined at first. We were a group of ten and we did not want to put him out. Besides, I figured he was just being polite. Later, after he made a phone call and insisted a second time that we stay with him, we agreed. We would sleep at his uncle's house as he was out of town and the house was empty and large enough to accommodate our group.

Before my friends arrived in Turkey, the parents of one couple in the group were uneasy. The thought of an American Christian visiting a Muslim country was frightful and they genuinely thought the couple's chances of being killed were fifty percent, an unfortunate fear based on stereotype, but one that makes sense given the unfamiliarity with Turkey among Americans and the standard fare American media produces concerning Muslims.

We opted for a detour on the way to the house, driving to the top of the mountain to take in the view. When we reached what I thought to be an impossible switchback curve in the road (with an unfenced cliff to our rear) I handed the keys to Ibo. He quickly and without trepidation made the "impossible" turn and sped up the mountain. He didn't slow down until we reached the top, and then he hit the gas and yelled "let's crash!," before slamming on the brakes near the cliff's edge. He laughed at that one. Hard.

Sixty-five percent, we joked to our friends.

We took in the gorgeous view of the Black Sea to our north and the Kaçkar mountains to our south. Ibo then motioned me over to the side of hill and pulled out his pistol. He fired across the valley and then we passed the weapon around so all the guys could take a few joy shots.

Seventy-five percent.

Later that night we settled into his uncle's house. Ibo left for a half-hour or so and returned with a bird. He promptly handed it to me and left again. So there I sat in a stranger's house, no Turkish friend around, holding a bird. This is my life, I thought. I live in Turkey. This stuff happens to me.

113

It wasn't the first time I had been invited to stay in a friend's home or the first time I fired joy shots from a pistol into the green Kaçkar beyond. It wouldn't be the last time I would sit around holding a bird, either. Guns and birds and friends and fun are just part of the Black Sea way of life, I was learning. I experienced such hospitality and friendship there that I knew I would return.

When Ibo returned we asked about the bird. He had mentioned going hawk hunting the next morning, so I thought this might be the bait bird. As much as my friends love guns, they do not use them when hawking and are quick to point out that no animals are actually hurt in the process of hawking. A bait bird, a small pigeon of sorts that is used to lure the hawk into a net, is caught using a trap, then blindfolded so that the bird can see down, but not straightforward or up. Tied to a stick, the bird is made to flutter around on one side of the net to attract the hawk, who dives from the clouds after the bird only to find himself tangled in a thin net. The hawker has a new pet. He will keep the hawk for a few weeks or months, or perhaps sell it or simply let it go. If its feathers are right he will use it to brag to his friends or strut through town with it. He will feed it egg and spend lots of time just sitting with it and his friends, just shooting the breeze.

The bird I was holding, however, was not the bait bird. When asked what it was, Ibo decided to just show us. So all the guys packed into the back of his truck and we sped up the mountain again. We came to his friend's parked van. After chatting for a few moments he demonstrated how to catch these small birds. First, he shined a large spotlight along the side of the mountain, this time in a pumpkin patch. Once in the spotlight, the bird was paralyzed by the light and he was able to catch it in a handheld net. He then stashed the bird in his messenger bag that was slung over his shoulder and contained his previous catches.

Lights, bags, birds. The whole thing sounded suspiciously like snipe hunting. And if I hadn't held the bird myself I'd have thought the same about this night. But this hunting is real, even if it yields no tangible benefits. They do it just for the fun of the chase, the catch. They don't eat the birds or really do anything with them. He said he'd release the birds soon. We did, however, pick a pumpkin from the patch and eat it—baked—as we sat out in the cool rain chatting late into the night.

The next morning all ten of us, eleven counting my then seven-month-old son, loaded up in Ibo's truck to go hawking. My son and I sat in the cab with Ibo, while everyone else piled in the pickup's bed. Halfway up the mountain an old man stood in the middle of the road, pistol drawn and pointed at us.

Eighty-five percent.

Ibo, with a smile on his face, drew his and pointed back. We stopped and they shared a few barbs in Lazuri, a minority language I did not understand. We laughed too, albeit nervously. I knew it was a joke, but still did not like that the barrel of the old man's pistol was still pointed in the cab at my son and me. I shielded him to my side.

We continued up the mountain and arrived at the designated spot. A few hawk blinds were built of sticks and straw and pine needles. The net was ready. I was pleased to learn that a key part of hawking is eating breakfast. Ibo keeps a table on top of the mountain, as well as a gas-powered stove to heat the tea. We talked and enjoyed the great outdoors and each other's company. A few friends joined us. Ibo and his friends did the hawking as we watched and tried to keep quiet. Unfortunately, silence is also key to hawking. And silence was hard to come by in a group of eleven Americans, including a baby. Our noise scared away a couple of hawks and we failed to net a single one.

But that didn't really matter. The heart of hawking is not in the hawks, but in the friendship. In the time shared with one another and with nature.

Ibo will climb this mountain almost every day during the warm months, sometimes netting a hawk, sometimes leaving empty-handed. But always leaving full. Asked why he does it, he responds simply. "Joy."

Zero percent.

11

Football Changed My Life

As I sat with Burak in a café in a business district of European Istanbul an unusual crowd gathered at the bus stop across the highway. A few minutes later, as we took our first sips of tea, we heard an explosion. Being from the dark corner of South Carolina I am not accustomed to hearing too many loud explosions, save the Fourth of July, the occasional meth lab in Marietta, or when a buddy says "hey y'all watch this." So I naturally got up to see what was going on since, according to comedian Cedric the Entertainer, that's what white people do. Burak, the linebacker, did not even flinch. He calmly noted that since none of the people crowded at the bus stop were running away everything must be fine. A news report later confirmed that a police bomb squad had detonated an abandoned bag, the contents of which were as harmless as arithmetic: school books. I pitied the poor kid who had to choose his excuse between "my dog ate my homework" and "the police blew it up on the outside chance that I was a terrorist."

It was no surprise that Burak did not flinch at the explosion. Not only are such events par for the course in Istanbul, but Burak is also a tough dude. Prior to playing football he was a kickboxer and fighter, a hobby he still enjoys. As a side job he provides security detail for concerts and other special events. And at age 36 he continues to pad up and play middle linebacker nearly thirteen years after his first practice as a university student. He still remembers the date—September 12, 2000—when he and fifty others filled the courtyard at Eastern Mediterranean University in North Cyprus for the team's tryout. No one was cut from the team at the tryout. They didn't have to be. Two solid weeks of running had a way of weeding out the weak. Those two weeks trimmed the roster to twelve players—just enough to fill a side—presumably because a population that treats cigarettes like mints generally prefers not to run wind sprints. I was consistently amazed at how many of our Stallions players happened to sprain an ankle just before the end-of-practice sprints.

Burak remembers that start date—and many other minute details of his football career—because the sport became his passion, part of his identity. He remembers his first loss, a 36-6 trampling at the hands of Ege University. "I was bleeding like hell, made our only touchdown as a safety, and [the loss] was like someone killed my mother," he recalls more than a decade later. Burak's two tattoos are a permanent reminder of those university glory days and how much his teammates meant to him. *EMU Crows Noster Nostri*, Latin for "our hearts beat as one," is inscribed over his heart. *H.C.L.*, which stands for the team motto of honor, courage, and loyalty, is inked on his chiseled left bicep. I asked him if the team was like a second family. He looked me dead in the eye and we had a moment worthy of a scene in *Rudy* or *Remember the Titans*. "Because I love my family I must say it is like a *second* family, but sometimes, believe me, it is like a family."

If Burak sounds a bit gung-ho or rah rah, even Tebowish, it's because he is just that. He is a football believer. The game and the teams have transformed him. Before he started playing football Burak was an individualist, at least when it came to sports. A fighter and a swimmer he succeeded and failed on his own. He was also a self-described roughneck, running with a rowdy crowd, fighting and partying like an "outlaw." His hair, disheveled and down his back, matched his lifestyle. He eschewed being likened as a hippie preferring to compare to himself to Seattleite grunge, more Nirvana than Grateful Dead. Today, he is newly married and sports a salt-and-peppered professional class haircut. On this day he ordered no food because the café did not have anything whole wheat. His outlaw days are far in the rear view.

Burak credits his football experience with giving him personal discipline and making him a tougher man. Sure, he was plenty *physically* tough before football—he fought for sport. But football gifted him a mental toughness that he previously lacked, a gift he considers the most important thing he gained from the game. Six o'clock in the morning practices trained him so that he is never late for work as an adult. The games taught him to never quit for there is always time on the clock, always another season. Talking to Burak, you get the feeling that football was something of a mentor, as if sports could take on the role of father figure.

When I began my interviews for this book I expected that the primary motivation for playing and the primary benefit from having played would be friendship, the brotherhood forged in the trenches of playing a non-traditional and physically demanding sport. I did not expect to find discipline so highly regarded by some pillars of Turkish football, especially after witnessing the utter lack of discipline from many current players. Seyfo, Burak's longtime friend and former rival and arguably the best player to ever don the Stallions uniform, also pointed to discipline as a motivation for playing.

"Football changed my life," Seyfo noted after openly admitting to living a wild, drug-infused lifestyle prior to joining the Stallions. Upon meeting the team he thought to himself that these were good guys and maybe he could change his life. He stopped drinking, smoking, and doing drugs and replaced those bad habits with eating healthy and working out. He even began to believe in God again, which he connected to working hard. "If you believe in God, you believe in hard work." Seyfo learned that to be a good player required him to be a good person first. The way to being a good person was through hard work and discipline, through believing and living clean. As a die-hard Patriots fan, Teddy Bruschi was his role-model. According to Seyfo, Bruschi was not the most talented or physically gifted player on the team, but because he was tough and a leader, he became the Patriots best player. Seyfo, who also played some linebacker in addition to stints at quarterback and running back, likened himself to Bruschi—not the most talented player, but the hardest worker.

Seyfo credited football with instilling in him a winning attitude, what he calls a football mentality. He remembered playing at Sakarya in the Stallions' second season needing a touchdown on the final drive to win. "In the huddle we promised each other that we'd win," Seyfo recalled to me. "And we drove down to win." He then recalled another game and another late-game victory. "If we have the ball, we don't leave the field without scoring," he implored his teammates. They scored and won. "Belief in each other is important," he said, "and we believe in our hearts." Though players do not earn any money for playing, even in the professional league, according to Seyfo they earn more valuable wages. They learn to be better people, how to be a good teammate, to fight for something and to defend something. "These things can help you in life," he said.

Hopefully, Burak and Seyfo are not the last of an old guard in Turkish American football. Seyfo fears that today's players lack the "football mentality" and play with the attitude that "we can't work too hard." Burak shares these sentiments. The sport will likely continue to grow, though the odds are slim it ever becomes mainstream. Yet, with any growth, the rewards for playing also increase. Sponsorships improve each season so potential money is on the table for top performers. With increased popularity comes increased prestige. As the sport grows it may begin to feel more corporate than club. The fear is that such rewards will outshine the intrinsic values found in playing for love of the game. The discipline, attitude, and community that an obscure band of brothers provides.

It is not certain how things will turn out for American football in Turkey. With the right visionary leadership it could take off. On a much smaller scale it could follow NASCAR in the United States—a regional subculture sport that goes national on the wings of corporate sponsorships and the element of danger that breeds interest. Or it could fizzle like XFL or the annual playoff hopes of the Cleveland Browns. This uncertainty is indicative of Turkey's national future as well. The burning question for geopolitical analysts is which way will Turkey go? Will it turn to Europe or the Middle East? Will it ally itself with the United States or Iran? Will its citizenry become more secular or more religious or something altogether different that defies simplified explanation? The future is murky like fog settling in over the Bosphorus, which is not to say it is bleak. Some people like fog. It is partly Turkey's uncertainty that makes it interesting.

But mostly it is the people that make Turkey interesting. It's eating sheep intestine sandwiches because your friend insists it is tradition. It's your center eating a hamburger on the sidelines. It's dancing on the team shuttle. It's Tebowing in the end zone. It's cuddling on the bus. It's yelling instructions on how to tackle in the winter rain. It's drinking hot tea afterwards and talking about the important things in life. It's moving 6,000 miles away from home and being accepted into a new family the very next day.

Turkey has its oddities, for sure. And like every country, it has its sins, too. But it also has its values. Coaching the Stallions for two years allowed me to learn these in ways I'll never forget and will always appreciate. I've learned community and friendship and leadership and love. I've learned how to welcome a guest and treat a foreigner. I've learned that Turkey defies stereotypes, and that in our own little way we all defy our stereotypes. We are more than what others say we are. Some hear "Muslim" and automatically think terrorist. Others hear "Turkey" and assume Middle Eastern desert. Neither are true, and I hope that through the lens of a game you have understood that, too. I hope you will see that despite our very real differences—whether they be cultural, religious or political—we can live together as neighbors without fear or suspicion or superiority.

And we can do it tailgating.

THANKS

Books, like lives, are never individual projects. I am thankful for the family and dear friends who share life with me and have helped make this book possible. I am thankful for my wife, Shannon, who moved six thousand miles away from home and lived this book with me. She was involved with the football team, gave feedback and ideas for the book and sacrificed much time with me to enable me to write. I am thankful for our son, Hudson, who brings much joy to our lives and for our soon-to-be-born child who will no doubt bless our family in countless ways.

I am thankful for the Stallions football players and other Turkish friends who welcomed our us into their *çevre*. Your kindness and friendship are treasured.

I am thankful for Coach Jay, Baba Zane and their families. Without them, we would have never moved to Turkey.

I am thankful for kind friends, Ryan and Grace, who read some *very* rough drafts of this manuscript and offered helpful feedback and corrections.

I am thankful for those who have written about Turkey before me and have done so much better. The "çay break" sections are a hat tip to Stephen Kinzer's *Crescent and Star*, one of the best books on modern Turkey.

I am thankful for you, the reader. I consider it an honor that you would take the time to read the book. I hope it was an enjoyable reading experience.

I am thankful for God who created the world and its people; who made us neighbors with the ability to love; who loved us; and who gave us words so that we could communicate in speech and in writing.

Rhett Burns, 2014

Made in the USA
Columbia, SC
28 March 2019